Weight Loss Without Willpower

Learn How to Programme Your Subconcious Mind for Sustainable Weight Loss Success

By Gillian Dalgliesh

© Gillian Dalgliesh 2024

Terms and Conditions
LEGAL NOTICE

Published by Babysteps Publishing Limited All enquiries to

kevin@babystepspublishing.com

ISBN- 9798884634275

This isn't your typical weight loss and motivation handbook. It's a game-changer in helping you wake up to how you've been unconsciously creating failure when it comes to your weight loss attempts.

It's a transformative experience designed to awaken you to the unconscious patterns that have contributed to your previous weight loss fails.The thoughts we put into our minds are far more important than the food we put into our mouths - It's our thoughts that dictate our success or failure.

This book will help you to release yourself from the prison of your own mind and programme your subconscious for success!

And it doesn't have to stop at weight loss - these powerful mind techniques can be applied to any area of your life!

Welcome to
Weight Loss Without Willpower
By Gillian Dalgliesh

I am so delighted you are reading this book, and before we get into the book, I'd like to briefly tell you Why I Wrote The Book, Why You Should Read The Book, What You'll Learn, and Who I Am.

WHY I WROTE THIS BOOK

At times, my life hasn't been easy – in mid-life, I unexpectedly experienced heartbreak, loss, hardship, homelessness and substance abuse - alcohol, as well as unhealthy eating. However, that's all a thing of the past because I learned how to use the power of my mind to change everything in my life for the better. And so can you! From the depths of utter despair, I realised that despite my outer reality being in a state of turmoil – my thoughts didn't have to support that! I started to imagine how I would feel if everything in my life was already resolved. This state of mind magically transformed my life and drew opportunities I could only have dreamed of towards me.

Initially, I used my wisdom and techniques to create courses to empower people who felt they were stuck in their lives; however, over the years, I trained in many clinical and healing modalities, including clinical hypnotherapy and life coaching, and I began to explore the power of the mind even more and to specialise in weight management. I've been helping clients with their weight for years now, and I've built up a catalogue of weight loss methods that are not only practical but, very importantly, give my clients insight into how they've been unknowingly negatively programming their subconscious. Most people don't realise that their subconscious mind isn't supporting them in their weight loss endeavours. In fact, it usually works against them because it reinforces old patterns that it believes they want.

So I've helped thousands of clients to sustainably change their weight loss mindset by giving them the awareness, insights, mindtools, language and techniques to harness the power of their subconscious minds in creating the weight and shape they've been unable to sustainably achieve in the past, and I'd like to help you too!

I wrote this book because when it comes to successful weight loss, studies have shown that 80% of people who shed a significant amount of weight will not maintain it. There are zillions of diets and weight loss clubs and methods out there, and yet most people are failing to lose weight and keep it off. So, what's missing between intention and success? The answer lies in the mind!

This book will enlighten you regarding how your previous thoughts and behaviours have been keeping you stuck in an endless repetitive cycle and pattern of unmet expectations and bring about awareness of how you can powerfully change all of that.

WHY YOU SHOULD READ THIS BOOK

- You've realised that simply relying on willpower, discipline, and self-control isn't the answer
- You've realised that the key to your lack of success lies in your mindset
- You're fed up with the repetitive cycle of yo-yo dieting
- You feel you've tried every diet and fad under the sun, and you're still not the weight and shape you want to be
- You're ready to sustainably and healthily lose weight

WHAT YOU'LL LEARN

- How to recognise three important WHY'S – WHY you want to lose weight, WHY you don't want to lose weight, and WHY you won't let yourself keep the weight off!
- How you've been unconsciously programming yourself for failure
- How to programme your subconscious mind for sustainable weight loss success
- How to re-wire automatic behaviour and break the spiral of yo-yo dieting
- Insights, self-awareness, mind tools and techniques to change your mindset forever

WHO AM I?

- I am a fully qualified therapist and certified life coach specialising in the areas of weight management and anxiety. I've been successfully working in the field of supporting clients to healthily and sustainably reduce their weight for the last 14 years.
- I have over a hundred 5-star Google Reviews.
- I hold a Batchelor of Arts from the University of Glasgow in Scotland.
- I also hold Diplomas in Clinical Hypnotherapy, Anxiety Management, Human Resources Management, and Theosophy, and I'm a certified Mental Health Practitioner.
- I'm also a Neuro Linguistic Programming Coach – That's NLP - trained in assisting clients to change their thinking and behavioural patterns, emotional states, and internal dialogue.
- I write for newspapers and magazines and have a regular blog on my website covering different aspects of building Emotional Resilience. My website is www.changewithgillian.com

- I regularly deliver inspiring talks & workshops and feature in motivational podcasts, and on radio.
- I also have a FaceBook group called 'Weight Loss Without Willpower'. And I'd urge you to join my community – I give weekly Lives, and I'm on there most days, so if you have any questions, you'll be sure to get an answer from me very quickly. You'll also be able to connect and share with other members on similar journeys.

So, let's get cracking on the book!

TABLE OF CONTENTS

HOUSE KEEPING

Firstly, there are six items of House Keeping.

1. There are **23 Chapters and Practical Exercises**

Each of the 23 chapters comprises a lesson and some practical exercises, which I call self-investment steps. The Self Investment Step techniques implement the learning from the Lesson.

The chapters can be read sequentially, 1, 2, 3, 4, etc, but you can also dip into them as you wish. However, I recommend that you complete each of the chapters and exercises.

I also recommend that you read the chapter in its entirety at least once before returning to complete the Self Investment Steps.

You'll likely find that you want to return to many of the chapters as you build up your personal catalogue of insights, awareness and transformative techniques and want to refer back to the wisdom I've provided.

2. **Recording your journey in your own 'Life Book' to accompany this program**

I would thoroughly recommend that you invest in a lovely notebook to journal your thoughts and feelings and use it to perform practical exercises.

I'd like to think that the cognitions and perceptions you make in this journey are so profound that this journal remains a constant companion with you going forward as you continue to grow and evolve in your life. I recommend that you journal your thoughts and feelings daily, if possible.

Obviously, you'll need a pen, and one of the exercises also asks you to use a red and a green pen. So it would be useful to have at least three pens, a blue or black one, and a red and green one, if possible.

A little tip that you may find helpful - I have one of those pens that are multi-coloured — at the top of the pen are four little sliders that enable me to choose black, blue, green or red. It means that if I am writing something and it's particularly meaningful, and I want to be able to find it again really quickly, I may write it in RED, and I use GREEN for healing or spiritual things. However, it's whatever works best for you.

A highlighter pen would also be useful for things that are particularly important to you.

In addition, there are some exercises where I suggest that you have some stickers that you can place around your workspace and living environment as reminders — I use little stars, but any kind of small sticker would work.

3. Making notes and recording electronically

When we're out and about, taking our journal with us is often impractical. So, I record on the Voice Notes on my phone if there's something important that I need to address or remember. Alternatively, you may prefer to record onto a voice transcription app so that you can make a print out of your audio to include in your Journal.

4. Creative Visualisation Meditation

This is a mindset meditation that uses light hypnosis, helps to programme your mind, and reinforces your conscious and subconscious beliefs about your success in achieving your goals. If you can, I recommend that you listen to the Meditation daily – preferably in the morning or before you go to sleep. If

2

you can't listen daily, then try to listen to it regularly throughout your week.

Using your mind and imagination to regularly see and feel yourself succeed in reaching your weight loss goals helps to programme our expectations that it can, is and will happen.

Obviously, only listen to it when it's safe to do so - please don't listen to it if you're driving, operating machinery or performing some other task that requires you to be fully cognisant.

You can find the link at www.changewithgillian.com/bookresources/

5. This program does not preclude you from being on what you've likely been referring to as a 'diet'; however, you'll learn that language has a powerful impact in programming our subconscious, so I prefer to use the phrase, 'healthy eating plan' instead of the word 'diet'.

6. Lastly, I have a **Facebook Group** to accompany the program – it's called Weight Loss Without Willpower. I encourage you to join as I do live calls every week, and I'm on there most days, so if you've got a question, please feel free to post it in the Facebook group, and I'll be able to respond to you very quickly. I hope I may look forward to welcoming you there!

NOTE – You'll be able to find many of the tables and lists that I refer to in the book as downloads on www.changewithgillian.com/bookresources/

So let's get started!!!!!!!!!!!!!!!!

Welcome to Chapter One on our journey …

CHAPTER 1

WHY <u>DON'T</u> YOU WANT TO LOSE WEIGHT?

The question I'm asking here might seem a bit of a paradox because you already believe that it's your desire to healthily, successfully and, very importantly, sustainably lose weight, and yet I'm now asking you, 'Why don't you want to lose weight?'. What can I mean by this? The answer is, "Why won't you let yourself keep the weight off?"

This may seem like a crazy notion, but the fact is, often, it's easier to stay as we are even though it's not what we want!

We all know HOW to lose weight; however, putting it into practice can be very different! As a result, many of us have a history of yo-yo dieting and repeated failures. Unfortunately, repeated failures tend to programme our minds negatively, and our subconscious gets the impression that this is what we want, reinforcing our negative beliefs! I know that sounds paradoxical, but that's often just how it is. Repeated failures affect our self-esteem, self-belief and self-value, which can become our default state when trying to lose weight. However, it does not have to stay like that! There is a MAGIC FORMULA, and it's simple: Your reasons WHY you want to lose weight have to be stronger than why you don't want to lose weight.

And by doing a bit of work on it, you can override the negative default state and repattern your mind!!!! Yes! Yes! Yes! You can!!!!!

When I think about the clients that come to me for weight loss, they nearly all fall into the same sort of type – they have busy, successful and fulfilled lives in so many ways. They are satisfied in so many areas of their lives and know success. Each one is different, but they can count success in a variety of areas in their lives – career, jobs, relationships, children, pets, holidays, sports, exercise, hobbies and health, to name but a few, but their one area of repeated failure is THEIR WEIGHT!

They're usually spinning plates in their lives as they're supporting many things and other people and are successful in these areas, but they cannot understand why they can't gain mastery over their weight loss.

For other people, it is simply a matter of being stuck in a groove and not recognising or acknowledging that certain fundamental beliefs need to be altered in order to bring about sustainable change.

However, I've found over the years that a universal major element in that lack of success is SELF-NEGLECT – not taking time for ourselves. Not making time to have that space where you can sit down and have that important inner dialogue with yourself where you can start to explore the elements of the thoughts and beliefs that are inhibiting your success in these weighty matters!

So this lesson is very much about PRIORITISING yourself – scheduling the ME TIME to think about yourself and your needs – no longer putting yourself at the bottom of the pile behind all the other things you've perceived as taking priority.

(A point to ponder – it's not uncommon for a client to tell me that they wouldn't dream of sending their kids to school without breakfast. But when I ask them if they themselves had breakfast, they'll often say, "No, I didn't have time". That's generally not the whole truth – the truth is usually - "No – I didn't prioritise my needs by creating the time to sit down and eat breakfast". Is it any surprise then that seeing an unhealthy snack later in the morning seems very appealing?)

SELF-INVESTMENT STEP:

Open your journal to a double-page spread.
On the left-hand page, write the heading WHY
On the right-hand page, write down the heading WHY NOT
On the left hand at the top of the page, write down a subheading (a) the reasons WHY you want to lose weight, and in the middle of the page, write a second sub-heading (b) Reasons WHY you keep failing.

The left side is the easy part –

The reasons Why I want to lose weight could be:

Physical health, mental health, living longer, mobility, looking better in clothes, more choice of clothes, a better role model for kids, attracting a new partner …
Write as many as possible and keep adding as you think of them.

The second part, Why I fail could be:

Too busy, not enough hours in the day, too stressed, looking after others, too tired, no willpower, I enjoy unhealthy food too much, it's hard to break bad habits around food and alcohol, it gives me comfort, I feel guilty if I give time to myself, I feel low, I'm rubbish, I'll start tomorrow

So go ahead and write your list of reasons.

And now the more searching part - and the most important part is WHY you DON'T want to lose weight. So make a sub-heading on the right-hand page (a) 'Reasons I don't want to lose weight". Initially, you may realise that you're writing down the same reasons that you wrote in the 'why I fail list':

Reasons why I don't want to lose weight:

Too busy, not enough hours in the day, too stressed, looking after others, too tired, no willpower, I enjoy unhealthy food too much, it's hard to break bad habits around food and alcohol, gives me comfort, I feel guilty if I give time to myself, I feel low, I'm rubbish, I'll start tomorrow

But these are all distractions – none of those reasons is a hard and fast solid reason for you being unable to sustainably lose weight.

It goes much deeper - what it boils down to is your relationship with yourself – much deeper thoughts.

So make another sub-heading entitled: (b) "The reasons I WON'T LET myself lose weight **and keep it off"**.

Here are some suggestions for you to ponder.

Some of these suggestions may seem irrational, but as you contemplate them, you may actually find that these deeper reasons resonate with you, and they may also even trigger other deep reasons that surprise you.

- I don't deserve to lose weight.
- Being overweight protects me.
- I feel safe within my crowd if I'm overweight
- What will happen to me if I'm not overweight?
- I identify as an overweight person.
- If I don't have to worry about my weight – what will I think and worry about instead?
- My needs aren't important
- Neglecting myself is safe because it's familiar
- I'm not worthy
- I'm just not good enough
- Prioritising myself doesn't feel right

And then, take the time to think about when you have been on diets, and they failed. Initially, you may find that the first set of reasons derailed you. However, when you reflect further, you'll realise that deeper reasons triggered the failure.

I call this step - **Recognition:**

This can take some time, and it's ongoing – so keep the journal near so you can add to it as things occur – this is VERY IMPORTANT!   This process is crucial in helping you to recognise the real reasons for the sabotage.

You owe it to yourself to really take the time to dig down deep – think about your typical behaviours, your triggers, what had been going on in your life that pushed you to sabotage your weight loss efforts, and why you were unable to stop yourself.

As you think deeper while making notes, other subconscious reasons may pop into your mind – events from the past and you realise you're still holding onto outdated negative emotions that are not serving you.
However, making this connection can help you acknowledge them, begin to process them, release them, and let them go! You could also start to realise how neglectful you've been of your own needs and how unkind and harsh you've been towards yourself.   Clearly, if that self-neglect and unforgiving self-talk were effective, then you wouldn't be here now starting to explore new ways of helping you to successfully and sustainably lose weight! It's time to change!

The processes in this lesson can give you fresh perspectives and help you to question and clear default emotions and reactions you've been holding onto that have been creating the repeated yo-yo dieting pattern.

As I said, you may very well find that you keep coming back to this step as valuable insights occur to you.

CHAPTER 2

DO YOU ACTUALLY BELIEVE YOU CAN SUCCESSFULLY LOSE WEIGHT?

In this lesson, I'm going to ask you to create two lists.

List A:

Think of areas in your life where you've enjoyed success. Here are some suggestions:
WORK/CAREER/BUSINESS – RELATIONSHIPS – EDUCATION – PARENTHOOD – FAMILY – SPORT – KNOWLEDGE – FILM BUFF – WELL READ – FINANCES – HOBBIES – DIY– HOME DECOR - GREEN FINGERS …

Think about and consider how you feel about yourself in your successful areas. What beliefs do you have about yourself in these areas? To begin with, choose one of these areas where you've achieved success, for example, Career. Perhaps your feelings about yourself in this area may be:

- I am able
- I feel successful
- I'm competent
- I am accomplished
- I can and have been able to manage setbacks and failures and take them in my stride.
- Nothing's perfect, but where I met failure or adversity or difficulty, I learned from my mistakes.
- I can manage my challenges
- I've been sustainably motivated

So … reflecting on those areas of achievement and success, what feelings do they give you about yourself? For example … do you feel

- Positivity
- Pride
- Power
- Satisfaction
- Motivated
- Self-belief, self-worth, self-esteem,
- Able
- Self-approving

These feelings are natural and justifiably support and encourage the successes that you are and have been experiencing in these areas, and they lead to a default state of self-belief and self-confidence.

As a result, it leads to a sense of positive expectation each time we encounter or experience these areas in our lives.

Positive Expectation!

Here's a little example of Positive Expectation: I wouldn't describe myself as an accomplished gardener, but I recently sowed some tomato seeds, and I planted them in full expectation that they'll grow into tomatoes, which I'll be able to enjoy and/or share. I didn't plant them with doubt, fear or uncertainty: I had every reason to know and expect that they'd grow to fruition because I wanted them to grow, and I knew that I'd be attending to their needs – regular water, sunlight, plant food, etc. It wouldn't happen overnight, so I knew that there'd no need for me to be disappointed if I didn't see seedlings breaking the surface of the soil the next day, the next week or even the week after – I simply planted them in the full and certain knowledge and expectation that they're going to grow because I'm caring for them and regularly giving them what they require.

My Mindset is:
I'm patient and have the belief that I'll see the happy and healthy evidence of that support, love, care and intention.

This is the same sort of mindset we want to embody when it comes to our weight loss intentions. Positive Expectation.

Now, we're going to create List B:

I'd like you to think about how you feel about your previous weight loss attempts. What beliefs are you holding onto about yourself? Here are some suggestions:

- Diets don't work for me – I've tried everything before
- I'm doomed to failure
- What's the point in trying – I always fail
- I'm big-boned
- It's hereditary – a lot of my family are overweight
- I just can't do it
- I don't deserve it – I feel guilt and shame. I'm not good enough
- I repeatedly lose weight and then put it all back on again, and more
- I start with optimism and commitment, but it never lasts
- I don't have the patience
- I don't really believe that I can sustainably lose weight

Wow! Now compare your thoughts, feelings, attitudes and beliefs about List A.
How does that make you feel?

The List B beliefs are very limiting, and almost without us realising it, they've become our autopilots – negatively guiding, influencing and reinforcing our thoughts, feelings and behaviours about ourselves regarding our weight loss attempts.
Now, what I'm about to say is very important to know – All our beliefs and behaviours stem from our thoughts. And those beliefs and behaviours create the outcomes in our lives.
The way our thought process affects the outcomes in our lives is this:
First of all, there's a **trigger** – the trigger could be something you've seen or heard – and this trigger gives us thoughts –

11

Therefore, we have a thought, and this very quickly leads to emotions and feelings, which almost instantly lead to words and pictures.

And these thoughts/emotions/feelings/words/pictures, when repeated regularly to ourselves, lead to our beliefs.

Our **beliefs** lead to our behaviours,
Our **behaviours** lead to habits
Our **habits** lead to the **outcomes in our lives**

Here's a simple example – the trigger is you seeing a cake.
Your thoughts are – that cake looks tasty.
Your words in your mind are – I know I like cake, and I fancy eating that cake.
Your behaviour is – you eat the cake
Your habit is – you often eat cake

The outcome is that regularly eating cake is part of the reason you're overweight, and it all started with a trigger (the cake), which led to a thought process reinforcing a belief, which led to action and outcome.

Your thoughts are a catalyst for self-perpetuating cycles. What you think directly influences how you feel and how you behave. So:
"If you think you can, or you think you can't, you're right!":
Thinking you're a failure makes you feel like a failure. And then, you'll act like a failure, which reinforces your belief that you must be a failure.

In a nutshell, what we focus on, we get more of – POSITIVE OR NEGATIVE.

We are all the product of the stories that we tell ourselves! However, these stories don't have to be you! They are just thoughts that became beliefs.

And when you consciously substitute positive thoughts and beliefs in the place of negative ones, such as

I am enough! I am valuable. I am confident. I can do it!

You change your story!!!!

Change your mind, change your life!

(Encouraging thought – Recently, I was speaking to a man who'd been a raging alcoholic for most of his life. He knew he had a problem and had tried to stop many times over the years and always relapsed. He'd been sober for the last three years when I spoke to him. I asked him what had changed after his final relapse – he said it was his attitude of mind. He said that it had dawned on him that he'd previously approached each period of sobriety with a sense of fear, doubt and uncertainty that he would be able to remain sober – he had a sense of expecting to relapse. When he realised this, he changed his thoughts and mindset to resolve and expectation of success. This became the default state of mind that supported him through the ups and downs of successfully living his life sober.)

(And by the way, you can find out more about Affirmations in a later chapter)

SELF INVESTMENT STEP

On a double-page spread, title the Left Page Limiting Beliefs in Red and title the Right Page Positive Beliefs and Intentions in Green.

Make a list of all your Limiting Beliefs on the left page (go onto the following pages if you need to)

Then, with each limiting belief about yourself, write a positive belief on the opposite side of the page.

When you've done this, with each Limiting Belief, say out loud - "**Cancel, Clear, Delete**", as you score it out and then say the positive belief that you've just written.

All the words we think and say have a vibrational energy that influences us, and when we state our thoughts and intentions out loud, it increases the impact and power of our convictions!!! Another powerful aspect of this is to state your positive intention out loud with joyous energy!!! Really enjoy this process!!!

As Limiting Beliefs pop up in your life, add them to the list and repeat the same process.

Here are some examples:

LIMITING BELIEFS CORRESPONDING POSITIVE BELIEFS

I always fail.	Failures are lessons. I have what it takes to succeed.
I can't stick to a diet.	I'm no longer living in my past. I am able to learn from previous experiences.
It's too much effort.	I have all the energy, focus and drive that I need to succeed.
It never works.	I choose to believe I'm capable of losing weight healthily and sustainably.
I'm easily discouraged.	I am applying the same level of expectation, success, and belief to my weight loss efforts as I have experienced in all the other successful areas of my life. I can do this! I am doing this! I am able to do this!

CHAPTER 3

GOALS AND TARGETS

Get SMART! And, very importantly, Anticipate Remorse Emotions!!!

Set yourself targets. You'll likely have an idea of your ideal weight loss goal. So, at the start of your journey, it's a good idea to break it down to measurable targets - S.M.A.R.T. targets – SMART is an acronym for:

Specific, Measurable, Achievable, Realistic, Timeframe

And you can use your Journal to record it all.

So initially, it's up to you to decide –

Specific: What is the specific weight or clothes size that you intend to achieve?

Measurable: How many lbs or kgs do you want to lose?

Achievable: You may feel that an average of 1-2lbs (or 1kg) per week is reasonable and achievable.

Realistic: How would it be practical to measure the weight loss – Weekly? Monthly? Using scales? Using a tape measure?

Timeframe: With an average weight loss of 1-2 lbs or a kg per week, what is the likely date you will achieve your goals?

Break down your journey into manageable steps, for example, a drop of 4/5lbs or 2.5Kg per month.

However, importantly, look at your calendar and see if any birthdays, celebrations, festivities or holidays are coming up and be realistic about how they may affect your eating and drinking habits. You may have to make allowances for those times – anticipation and planning are essential in supporting this weight loss action.

Advance Planning
As you successfully achieve each stage, plan in advance how you are going to celebrate it!

Record it in your Journal – a massage, cinema outing, pedicure …
BE KIND TO YOURSELF – Make sure to celebrate your successes!!!! It is SO IMPORTANT to congratulate yourself! Say it out loud!

A vital strategy to have prepared in advance is **Anticipating Remorse Emotions.**
This is a very important step concerning cancelling out remorse emotions:

It's where we add a dynamic to the SMART method that many people don't consider.

Being realistic, there is a possibility that you won't make a target, so in your Journal, write down how you will talk to yourself in that scenario. In this way, you have a powerful pre-prepared script to cancel out the remorse emotions before they take hold because those feelings often lead to sabotage.

Anticipating a setback: Creating your Personal Resilience Toolkit.

- Prepare in advance a note of what you have successfully achieved so far (keep updating this list)

16

- Look for reasons that could have stalled your progress but didn't – write them down.
- Write the words of encouragement, positivity and support that you'd need to hear if you stalled
- Highlight things you've already recorded in Steps 1 and 2 and other future steps that would be useful insights to consider here.

If you find you've stalled:

- Read through your Personal Resilience Tool and add to it.
- Speak it to yourself out loud using the sort of encouraging language you would use with a friend!
- Speak to yourself in the 3rd person – this is a psychological tool for disassociating with the sense of failure or remorse.
- Use humour to lighten the mood.
- Think the bigger picture – this is a kick in the shin; it's not a broken leg.

I cannot overestimate the importance of having this pre-prepared script. It's your parachute. A safety net.

SELF INVESTMENT STEPS

A. In your Journal, write out your Goals and Targets in the SMART format.

S.M.A.R.T.	
Specific goal	To become ten stones (64kg/140lbs)
Measurable	To lose two stones (24lbs/ 11kg)
Achievable	To lose 2lbs around (1kg) per week
Realistic	I'll weigh myself once a week.
Time Frame	Record your start date And your anticipated end date Note any likely celebrations, festivities, holidays, etc, that may affect your progress

B. Record in your Journal how you're going to mark and celebrate each successful stage in your journey.
C. Create your Personal Resilience Toolkit: Record in your Journal the things you're going to say to yourself if you don't make a target.

CHAPTER 4

VISUALISING

**OUR IMAGINATION IS AN IMPORTANT TOOL -
It's more powerful than knowledge.**

As I mentioned previously, a creative visualisation meditation accompanies the book. You can find it at
https://changewithgillian.com/bookresources/

Visualisation is a common-sense success strategy that can keep you motivated and focused to achieve your weight loss goals. It's about applying our powerful gift of imagination to our motivation, faith and confidence.

It's said that everything we create happens twice – first in our imagination and then in our actual lives. So, allowing the image of seeing ourselves as our ideal weight and shape to exist in our mind accelerates it into our reality. It makes our journey easier.
But if we can't see and feel ourselves as successful, then it can diminish our positive progress.

Regular visualisation helps you focus your mind on what you want and activates the creative powers of the subconscious mind, motivating it to work harder at creating successful outcomes. And what really turbo-boosts the creative force of your visualisation is imagining how it would FEEL to already be your ideal weight and shape!

Because the essence of manifestation doesn't just lie in pictures and words but with the vibrational energy of feeling that something already exists! The excitement, the gratitude and appreciation of already having something you want in your life.

I call this technique **Conscious Creation.**

So, take a moment to imagine how your future self would look. In your mind, see yourself in a full-length mirror. See yourself as your ideal weight and shape. What clothes are you wearing? What shoes have you on? How does your hair look? Use all your senses – are you wearing a perfume or scent you can smell? Can you taste a lipstick, lip salve or even something you've just eaten or drunk?

Look at your face – see your eyes shining, your skin is beautiful, your smile is radiant! How would you feel? How confident would you be? How would you be holding yourself? How would you move?

Imagine that this has already happened!

Allow yourself now to feel joyful and happy as you see yourself in the future!

Start to experience yourself as peaceful, happy, content, joyous, strong, healthy, powerful, successful and vibrant ….. !!!! Because your subconscious mind doesn't know if what you're experiencing is real or not, it simply responds to where you're putting your focus and gives you more of the same. As I mentioned, by regularly focusing on what you want as if you already have it, your subconscious will help engineer the appropriate thoughts, words and behaviours to support your success!

SELF INVESTMENT STEPS

(1)
Commit to yourself that you will do this visualisation daily – as soon as possible after you get up. By visualising in the morning, you are setting your emotional energy and resilience for the rest of the day. And remember that each time you

visualise yourself as your perfect weight and shape, you are one step closer to its fulfilment!!!!

(2)
To aid you with the mental imagery, as I mentioned previously, I have recorded a visualisation to assist you in seeing yourself as your ideal self. I call it the Future Present Visualisation, for it helps to enable you to bring the future into your present as if it already exists. Listen to the visualisation daily or regularly.

(3)
And now follows a **Mind Magic Method** – a simple yet powerful technique to change your life. For me, it's one of the hidden truths of the Universe, and it's a gift to yourself!

If you would like to engineer a way of being that will create a daily positive flow into your life, list how things will be once you are your ideal weight and shape – what things will change, and how you feel? Be clear about it all and pump up that positive energy – being your ideal weight and shape would bring so much happiness, joy and satisfaction! Imagine how you'd be feeling once it's already happened!

And now, I want you to place little stickers around your house and workspace, and whenever you come across one of these stickers, think about whether what you are presently saying, thinking and feeling is bringing you any closer to the optimal weight and shape you want to be. Remember – your words, thoughts and feelings create your reality!

When you've caught yourself, a few times, talking, thinking or feeling negatively and unproductively: First, stop being surprised about any lack of progress in your journey, and secondly, at the very moment you realise how often you've been defaulting to a negative or resigned state of mind and change it back to an emotionally buoyant and optimistic one, you start the process of awakening to a new mindset and reality. By repeatedly changing your mindset this way, you're training your mind to support you in creating what you want.

The only difference between an aware person and an unaware person is that the aware person creates their reality consciously, and the unaware person creates their reality unconsciously and then likely wonders why their expectations aren't being realised.

CHAPTER 5

STRATEGIC REFLECTION

Recognise and stop repeating the same old patterns.

Since you've bought this course, it's very likely that you'd like to reduce your weight and already have a history of failures. Well, here are some relevant statistics:

64% of people in a recent survey said that they try to lose weight "all or most of the time".

80% of people who successfully lose at least 10% of their body weight will gradually regain it to end up as large as or even larger than before they went on a diet!

And here's an interesting piece of information: In many people's minds, 'Diets are not associated with long-term weight loss.'

So what's going on? Why are so many people failing to lose weight?

What's going on in your world? What's your weight loss history?

Let's jump straight to the **SELF INVESTMENT STEP**.

I'd like you to create six columns in your Journal on a double-page spread.

The headings are:

Method

Age
Situation
Significant event(s)
Time of year/season
Reason for lack of success

Under 'Method'

Make a list of what you have tried in the past.

Diets / Fads / Exercise / Fasting etc –

Think hard about this and create a very comprehensive list. For each item on your list, try to remember details and information to fill in under the other headings. For example - What age were you at the time? What was your situation: were you at school, a student, employed, on holiday, experiencing parenthood, etc? Were there any significant events occurring? What time of the year was it? Was the season relevant?
And under the final column – Reason for lack of success – take the time to think about each one in turn and see if you can identify why they may have worked for a while, what halted them, or why they didn't work at all.

This will give you so much more insight and awareness, and perhaps even a pattern will evolve – i.e. I was doing well and in control of my eating, and then every time there was a night out, a party, a celebration, time of the month, a stressful event, etc., I lost my way, and it was in for a penny in for a pound!

Perhaps you can recognise life events, stressors or triggers that derail you.
Maybe you can recognise people who have derailed you.

Maybe you can recognise a pattern in the times of the year or the seasons.

By giving yourself the time to do this reflection, you can gain awareness and insight - perhaps discovering patterns - which can give you a fresh perspective in creating self-supporting strategies to give you sustainable weight loss.

SELF REFLECTION

I'd like to feel that by now, in this programme, you'll be starting to become more conscious that successful, healthy, progressive and sustainable weight loss is very much a whole life/holistic self-awareness, process and experience – it's not just about restricting the foods you eat.

It's also very much about ENJOYING THE PROCESS of doing the detective work!

Of investing time and energy in yourself and using these tools to develop a mindset which will continue to support you in achieving your intended weight and shape.

Recalling your weight loss endeavours and diet history will likely take effort and be time-consuming. But it is time well spent in investing in yourself.

If you stop and consider the amount of time you've spent in the past thinking about food, you may shock yourself! A lot of my clients tell me they obsess about food – thinking almost constantly about what they're going to eat, when they're going to eat, how much they're going to eat, negotiating with themselves with thoughts like – "if I don't eat this, then I can have that", "if I skip breakfast, then I can eat more at dinner", and constantly counting calories.

And then there's the relentless remorse talk, "Oh, I shouldn't have eaten such and such", "Oh, I feel rubbish", and "I'm so disappointed in myself"…. It fills their minds.

The Magic Key

So, when you consider all the time and effort you've put into creating a weight and shape you don't want, I'd like you to know that once you start consciously putting a similar amount of time, thought, focus and energy into what you do want, then you have discovered one of the magic keys to release you from the prison of your own mind! This is a method of positively and powerfully programming your subconscious by re-writing your internal script so you stop repeating the same old patterns. Initially, it won't come easily, but with awareness, focus, commitment, and enjoyment, it becomes your default state more and more!

And part of the magic is that this can also support you in all other aspects of your life!

STRATEGIC REFLECTION CHART

Method	Age	Status: school, Student, Working, Parent,	Significant event	Season	Lack of Success Reason
The Chocolate Bar Diet	18	Student		Summer	I very quickly got fed up with Chocolate Bars
Slimming Club	23	Working	Bridesmaid at a friend's wedding	Spring	I lost 12lbs to fit into my dress. I started eating and drinking as I liked at the wedding and carried on. I'd replaced the weight in a few months and more.
Slimming Club	24	Working	Foreign holiday	Summer	I lost 6lbs to go on holiday. Therefore, I felt justified in having a blow-

					out on holiday, quickly replacing the weight, and more.
5:2 Diet	25	Working		Winter	I hit a plateau after losing a few lbs, got bored, gave up
Intermittent Fasting	26	Working	Festive Season	Winter	I tried losing weight before the start of the Festive Season. I found I got too hungry on this diet, so I eventually gave up. The festive season came along, and I had added 5 lbs by January.
Low Carb Diet	26	Working	January	Winter	I tried to be very strict with myself, but January can be a miserable month. I couldn't fit my clothes, I felt upset, and I went out with my chums to cheer myself up – alcohol and pizza, etc. I just gave up – promised myself I'd start properly from 1st February.

CHAPTER 6

YOU'RE NOT ON A DIET

How the language we use can work against us.

Our notion of a "diet" generally implies that it's something restrictive and is usually associated with words like willpower, discipline, self-control, denial, deprivation and a set of scales. These are not the jolliest or most pleasant of travelling companions. In fact, if you get on the weight loss wagon and these are your companions, then – as you may have experienced in the past – one or a combination of them will likely let you down, push you off the wagon, and you'll land on the hard rocky road of despondency feeling wretched and miserable!

Another implication of the word 'diet' is that there's a timescale to it – It's got a beginning and an end: You've decided that you're heavier than you'd like to be, estimated how much weight you'd like to lose, calculated roughly how long it'll take you to lose the weight, and decided that you'll restrict your food intake in some way and remain faithfully focused on your successful result until you've achieved your weight loss goal - and then you'll return to normal eating habits. If only it were that simple.

Well, here's some news for you – you probably don't have your subconscious mind supporting you in your weight loss endeavours. In fact, it's almost certainly likely to be working against you because it'll reinforce the old patterns that it believes have kept you safe and in your comfort zone and that those are what you want. So let me tell you about …

Unconscious Subconscious Sabotage

Our subconscious is all about keeping us safe and keeping us alive. It's our loyal, faithful, devoted servant. It's constantly running programmes to control how we behave, including what we eat. It's there to support us and look after us, and if it perceives that we're denying ourselves something that it believes we enjoy, for example, chocolate, and that we have a sense that we are 'forbidding' ourselves this treat, the subconscious can jump on board and sabotage our endeavours – not through malice – it just thinks that it is giving you what you want. It doesn't possess reason – it just responds to your historical patterns and where you're placing your focus. Unless it's reprogrammed via different thought patterns, it doesn't know that you are trying to change your eating habits. It just knows that you have always or regularly eaten chocolate – especially in times of stress or reward (if that is your habit) and it sends out the signals for you to want to eat chocolate. Hence the sabotage!

In fact, I contend that, oddly, the subconscious can sometimes even orchestrate scenarios in our lives whereby we feel stressed about something and, therefore, we feel that we need 'comfort' or we have accomplished something very well, so we feel the need to reward ourselves. Either way, the subconscious steps in to re-create the previous patterns and delivers the obstructive pattern!

Programming our Subconscious for Success

So, first of all, we want to re-write our internal script with the notion that we're not on a diet. We're actually adopting healthy lifestyle changes around what and how we eat and - very importantly - how we feel about ourselves and what we tell ourselves. As I've mentioned in a previous chapter, around 80% of people who lost weight on a diet, put it all back on again and usually more. Diets are generally short-term because we're on them for a reason. I'm advocating lifelong lifestyle choices that revolve around self-care and self-support. We're not denying ourselves anything; we're simply choosing to eat differently and more healthily.

An important factor in this is the language we choose to speak to ourselves and others. Our language helps us to create new attitudes and beliefs that the subconscious will support.

The SELF INVESTMENT STEPS are about **Re-writing the Language**

It always amazes me that making small changes in our language has such awesome power to influence success and failure in our lives! So here are some valuable insights on how your choice of words can reprogramme your subconscious:

The word Diet v Healthy Eating Plan

Replace the word diet with 'healthy eating plan':
Diets imply restriction and can be generally considered negative things. As I mentioned in Chapter 5, diets are generally not associated with long-term weight loss.
On a healthy eating plan, you are not denying yourself anything. You are choosing to eat more healthily.

Diets tend to have a timescale. A healthy eating plan is a lifestyle choice and can last forever.

The word Normally v Used to, Previously

Replace the word "normally" with "used to" or "previously" – this reinforces the subconscious programming, for example:
"I would normally have biscuits with my tea."

BECOMES

"I used to have biscuits with my tea".
"Previously, I had biscuits with my tea".

'Used to' and 'Previously' imply that this habit of having biscuits with your tea is a thing of the past. They disassociate us from the ownership and belief that this is still our habit.

Positive Intentions v words such as Don't, not, no …

Another change to your vocabulary is substituting positive language where you would previously use negatives. The subconscious mind cannot easily process the word 'don't' or things stated in the negative, such as no or not.

For example, if you see chocolate and tell yourself, "I don't want that". "I don't need that", "I'm not going to have that". I know it sounds bizarre, but your subconscious mind cannot hear the 'don't' and is actually hearing you say, "I want that", "I need that", or "I'm going to have that".

The answer here is to alter the language to a more positive statement.

You see the chocolate, and you say,

"I can do without that".
"I'd rather choose something healthier."
"I am happy to choose something different – perhaps fruit."
"I'd prefer something healthier."
"I am content to do without".
"I'm pleased to resist."

Using the word Could instead of Should/Shouldn't

Saying to yourself that you "should have or shouldn't have" done something is harsh and can be very scolding, unhelpful, and diminishing and can lead to the repetition of old patterns. Re-phrasing with a 'could' is generally so much kinder, more helpful, insightful, and supportive, and it opens us up to alternative possibilities going forward and helps us explore our motivations and how we can make changes.

For example:
"I shouldn't have eaten that cake!" =
"I could have resisted eating the cake, but I didn't. Therefore, I wonder why not?"

"I should have eaten fruit instead of the chocolate" =
"I could have chosen fruit instead of chocolate, so let me think about what I was thinking and what was going on that made me opt for the chocolate."

"I shouldn't have done such and such."
"I could have acted differently in that situation, but I didn't, so what was really going on at the time?"

"I shouldn't have said such and such."
"I could have said something else instead. It's too late now, but how could I act/say something differently in the future?

'Could' opens up the possibility of gentle questioning – exploring reasons, situations, histories, wants, needs, etc., that can help us re-frame our impulses. It is a much kinder, gentler and self-supporting frame of mind. It helps to create a self-supporting inner coach to encourage and sustain our wellbeing. **Changing the word Need to = Choose to, Ready to, Open to, Able to**

Instead of telling yourself things like,
"I need to lose weight."
"I need to stay focused",
"I need to stay on this weight loss path."
change your language to
"I choose to reduce my weight."
"I'm ready to lose weight and change my thoughts and eating patterns "
"I choose to change my thoughts and eating patterns."

"I'm open to a new way to lose weight."
"I am learning to stay focused."

'Need to' is fear-based, and it also implies past failures and doubts that you'll stay on the path. It's a white-knuckle ride!

'Choose to", "Ready to", "Open to", and "Learning to" are peaceful, self-empowerment and confidence-based and open us up to having belief in our positive choices and actions.

The word And v But

You may be aware of saying to yourself things like:

"I hope that I can stay on my diet this time, **but** I've failed in the past."
"I really want to lose weight and keep it off, **but** it'll likely be a challenge."

The word 'but' acts as a block to what you want. Your subconscious is hearing a linguistic obstacle as 'but' implies opposition to your intention and a conflict in regards to your desire. The 'but' implies doubt, so you haven't got the full force of your subconscious supporting you in your intention.

To avoid the potential negative impact of 'but,' it's a good idea to replace it with the word 'and'.

For example:

"I hope that I can stay on my diet this time, **and** with the insights this course gives me, there are so many reasons to believe I can!".

"I really want to lose weight and keep it off, **and** I'm excited about the positive changes I'm making!".

The word 'and' links the two statements with a much more constructive tone and helps the positivity of the intention flow.

The small but powerful word, 'Yet.'

Have you ever said to yourself, "I can't do this"?   "I can't successfully keep the weight off".
"I can't stick to a diet".
Remember your subconscious is literal and non-judgemental, and what you're doing is giving it instructions, and you're unwittingly setting up an unconscious belief that you're destined to fail at every weight loss endeavour.
The word 'yet' is a powerful and positive linguistic tool because it implies potential, progress and future success.
"I can't do this yet". "I can't successfully keep the weight off yet". "I can't stick to a diet yet".

By adding the word 'yet,' you're implying you're open to change and referencing a positive mindset of motivation and persistence so that your subconscious knows there's still potential for it to happen.

Acceptance and Self-Permission

Accept that it would be unrealistic to never be able to eat treats while you are reducing your weight and shape and that you can comfortably include them in your eating plans from time to time – then plan when you intend to have them – perhaps once a week, perhaps a Saturday night?

By giving yourself permission to have treats from time to time, you'll find it a lot easier to stick to a healthy plan.
The subconscious will get the message, help, and support you to stay the distance.

CHAPTER 7

MOVEMENT AND EXERCISE

Actualise your good intentions!

The 'eat less, move more' model suggests that the benefit of exercise is that it uses up calories and helps you achieve a calorie deficit. In reality, physical activity doesn't inherently lead to weight loss, but certain types of exercise can aid weight loss.

Actually, we don't have to exercise to lose weight, but exercise is often advised for weight loss. However, what people should really aim for is fat loss. If you simply reduce your calorie intake to lose weight without exercising, you'll probably lose muscle as well as fat.

Exercise helps you lose weight by burning mostly fat; diet alone won't do that, and exercise can also help you develop muscle suppleness and flexibility. In addition, because muscles take up less space than fat, exercise will help your clothes fit better. Exercise also helps boost your metabolism, meaning you burn more calories all day and makes you feel better by releasing endorphins - giving you that virtuous feeling when you're finished!

What's important is that we choose something that we enjoy. Otherwise, our motivation can slip.

So here are ten different exercise choices:

Walking is one of the best exercises for weight loss, especially power walking. Plus, you're outdoors in the fresh air.

Jogging and running are great exercises to help lose weight.

Cycling
Weight training

HIIT – High-Intensity Interval Training – alternating between periods of high and low intensity.

Swimming

Yoga

Pilates

Gym classes

Investing in a personal trainer – even if it's just once a month for them to show you precise exercises.

You may be a gym bunny, and even in Lockdown, you'd continued to exercise, so how about changing it up – alternating routines, checking out the internet for alternative workouts, etc? Increase your weights, increase your intensity?

But for those of us who are less active, here are some suggestions:

Set yourself a goal – exercising can be hard, but if you keep your mind on the goal you're looking to achieve, it can help carry you over the tough times.

If you're working from the office, make a pledge to yourself that during your working hours, you will involve more movement in your day – be specific – what will it be?

Many of us are now working a lot from home – so firstly, decide what sort of activity would be reasonable for you – it could be a walk around the garden, going up and down the stairs, stretching, planking, lifting weights, dancing to the radio … and make a pledge to yourself you'll do it!

Always take the stairs.

Set a timer on your phone to get up and move – it could be once an hour or a couple of hours.

Each time the timer rings, leave what you are doing, get up and perform your chosen activity – Obviously, if you are on a Zoom or phone call, you may have to delay it!

If you can, invest in a Fitbit or use some other way of recording your activities, steps, health, heart rate, sleep, etc, as well as setting yourself challenges.

SELF INVESTMENT STEPS

Print out the Weekly Planner that you'll find on my website at https://changewithgillian.com/bookresources/ and write down what exercise you'll do that week, when you'll do it, and for how long. Block it out and colour-code it.

By actually writing things down, you're getting them out of the vague soup of good intentions swirling around in your head and seeing them reflected back at you in black and white. This very simple act shows commitment to yourself and is a valuable tool in programming your subconscious mind to support you with these good intentions.

Stick the planner up on your fridge or kitchen cupboards or somewhere else where you'll see it regularly – this reinforces intention and commitment and, very importantly, reinforces our sense of accountability, self-approval and self-congratulations. These are inspiring and motivating emotions!

By the sheer physicality of writing your exercise windows down, you're creating the space in your mind and physically committing yourself. I do recommend you colour code your exercise windows so they stand out from the other things in your week. Always make them the same colour, as this registers instant recognition and consistency in your mind.

Record in your Journal if you've exercised that day and how it made you feel!!!

Self-Celebration!!!

CELEBRATE YOU!!!!! I can't stress this enough! Take the time to compliment yourself, say out loud, "Well done, I am so totally awesome!!!!" Your subconscious is your obedient servant and will resonate this to you – the more you say it, the more you'll believe it, and the quicker it can become your default state!!!!!

At a deep level, congratulating yourself expresses self-value and self-worth and boosts your self-esteem. Self-esteem is a HUGE motivator in keeping us on track!!!!

CHAPTER 8

AFFIRMATIONS

Warning! They can work against us!

I will be talking about positive and negative affirmations in this module, starting with the negative ones.

Negative Affirmations

A lot of us think that an affirmation is a positive statement that we have to keep remembering to repeat to ourselves and that the more we repeat it, the more we'll believe it, and it can, therefore, help us to reprogramme negative thoughts and behaviours – this is true.

However, the reality is that we are far more likely to be unwittingly programming ourselves every day with negative affirmations!!!! Our beliefs are simply our thoughts that we put into words and tell ourselves regularly. So if your beliefs about yourself are something like, for example: "I can't stay on a diet", "I'm useless at losing weight", "I've no willpower", "I'm so disappointed in myself", "I can't do this", then it's likely you'll regularly repeat these types of statements to yourself and others and what you're actually doing is unconsciously negatively affirming these beliefs and programming your subconscious with them.

As I've mentioned, whatever your subconscious mind hears you repeating regularly is what it believes you want and will give you more of.

So let's think about **Mind Training** – and it's very simple - it just takes awareness and practise.

All you need to do is:

(a) recognise these statements each time you make them, and
(b) counter them with a positive affirmation

Let's consider, therefore, **Positive Affirmations.**

Positive affirmations are supportive statements that can help you to challenge and overcome self-sabotaging and negative thoughts. Even if you initially don't feel like you properly believe the statement, if you repeat these statements often, you will start to believe in them, and you'll start to make the corresponding positive, lasting changes.

Advertisers and behavioural psychologists know this to be true. Advertising is a hugely successful multi-billion dollar industry because advertisers know the power that repeated messages have in influencing people's choices. They know that **repetition breeds belief.**
Affirmations are amazingly powerful ways of raising our mood, raising our spirits and giving us emotional resilience.

When used consistently and correctly, positive affirmations profoundly influence your mindset, which can increase your motivation, energy, and enthusiasm towards achieving goals and/or breaking negative habits.

As I mentioned, even if you don't think you can initially 100% believe them, by regularly repeating them to yourself, your subconscious mind starts to believe them to be true and gives you the corresponding positive behaviours!

But, all the same, here's a technique you can use to more readily accept the truth of your affirmation from the outset. For example, say you want your affirmation to be "I am my perfect weight and shape", but you know in reality that you're not there yet. Therefore, very importantly, you can add words such as:

"I am **in the process of** becoming my ideal weight and shape".
"I am **learning how to** become my ideal weight and shape".
"I am **teaching myself how to** become my ideal weight and shape".
"**I can now learn how to** love myself in the process".

Adding these words makes the affirmation believable because you may not have reached your ideal goal yet, but it's true that with your correct intention, you're on your way.

Important note:

Keep the affirmation in the present tense: Rather than saying, "I want ... ", be sure to say: "I am ...." or "I can .... ".   Saying, "I want .. "or "I will ... " implies something in the future, and that implies doubt that you'll get what you want.   So it's important to ground it in present tense language as this is training your subconscious mind to think in terms of what you already are and what you already have, rather than it being a projection of something you want in the future.

SELF INVESTMENT STEPS

Choose your affirmation(s)
Decide how you're going to include your affirmations in your daily life.
   (a) How are you going to remember to do them regularly throughout your day?
   - I set a reminder on my phone.
   - I have also got into the discipline of repeating them to myself on my way to the bus stop, when I'm at the traffic lights in my car, in the shower, when I'm exercising, when I'm cooking, clearing up, doing the housework ... wherever, the more you do it, the more it becomes your habit.

(b) How often are you going to repeat them each day? I recommend it as much as conveniently possible.

(c) You can say them internally or out loud. Whichever is most appropriate.

(d) As things change in your life, you can change and modify your affirmations.

The Power of the Written Word and The Power of Sound

Consider writing your daily affirmation on a few Post-it notes and sticking them in places where you'll regularly see them. And when you see them – say them out loud!!!! Writing alone is powerful enough, but if you turn these statements into the powerful vibration of sound, they can become your reality even faster!!!

Say them like you mean them! Say them with gusto! Use your body – throw your hands up, punch the air! Own the powerful feelings!!   Get excited about them like they've already happened!

Give some thought to what Affirmations would be good for you. Here are some suggestions:

1. I believe in myself and my ability to succeed.
2. I have hope and certainty about the future.
3. Everything I eat is to nourish and strengthen my body and mind.
4. I'm doing the best I can, and I accept mistakes and learn from them.
5. I exercise to enjoy a strong body. I love the feeling that exercise gives me.
6. It doesn't matter what other people say or do. What matters is how I choose to react and what I choose to believe about myself.
7. Making small changes is becoming easier. I enjoy the feeling of well-being these changes are giving me.

8. I choose to let go of all negativity that rests in my body and mind.
9. I choose to be positive and surround myself with positive people.
10. I accept the past and know that I have the ability to build a positive future.

You can find a free list of 30 Daily Affirmations on my website at https://changewithgillian.com/bookresources/

Importantly - Record in your Journal at the end of the day how your Affirmations are making you feel and the changes you're noticing.

CHAPTER 9

TRIGGERS

There are two parts to this chapter.

Triggers - Part One

TRIGGERS – we all have them!

This is your time to make a list of everything that triggers a negative emotional response in you … here are some examples - work, colleagues, family members, friends, relationships, clutter, deadlines, unfinished tasks, thinking negatively about your weight, bingeing, loneliness, fear of the future, money, guilt, boredom, bad habits, and so on …

When we encounter a 'trigger', we generally autopilot to a negative state, and that can become our learned behaviour. It lowers our mood and can lead to unhealthy food choices.

However, by thinking about your triggers before they occur, you're allowing yourself to 'head them off at the pass'. Give yourself some already anticipated responses that you can put into place before the negative emotions associated with the triggers can derail you. By doing so, the triggers lose their emotional charge. When triggers lose their emotional charge, they're no longer triggers; they're just occurrences for you to respond to rather than react to.

As I keep repeating, how you feel is largely determined by what your beliefs are. Your beliefs influence how you see things and how you react. So when you're feeling stuck, if you can change the way you approach your stuckness, you'll often find a way to move forward.

Perspective is everything, and if you can find a way to change yours, then you may find a new view of a trigger that is very different from what you've been experiencing.

Seven Tips For Changing Our Perspectives:

1. Look for the positive in each situation. Often, we tend to see events that impact us negatively in the worst possible light and get stuck with that view... However, with a bit of self-awareness, we can become the half-full glass rather than the half-empty one! It may take effort, but it's worth it.

2. Allow the improbable to become possible... Acknowledge your present way of thinking about a situation, imagine your perfect outcome, and then daydream about that becoming your reality. Really enjoy this - let your thoughts wander and allow your subconscious to give you inspiration, ideas, answers and solutions!

3. Change your self-perception ... we've all heard the phrase 'the grass is always greener on the other side'. This phrase means that the things we don't have seem better than the things we do have. Time to get the powerful Gratitude Tool working and start counting your blessings and acknowledging what you do have!!!! *The grass is always greener where you water it!!!*

4. Keep an open mind ... have a willingness to try new things or to hear or consider new ideas. Consider listening to podcasts, YouTube videos, Ted Talks or googling information in order to hear other people's points of view.

5. Change your perception of other people – believe me, despite outward health and success, most of us struggle

with something or other that we keep hidden. However, it's often the case that if someone snaps at us or we encounter unpleasantness from someone, we take it personally. It eats us up, and we often blame ourselves, thinking that it must be our fault. Take a philosophical attitude and remember that they may well be experiencing personal challenges right now. Compassion and kindness cost us nothing and can mean a great deal to someone else.

6. Breathe in - take as much air as you need. Fill your lungs and then breathe out. Don't worry about taking more than your fair share. There's plenty to go around. Thank goodness for that. It's vital stuff. Yet we take it for granted. We focus on what we lack (rather than being grateful for what's in abundant supply). Take a moment to think about other things that are plentiful in your world. Hope. Love. Comfort. If there aren't as many of these as you'd like, start acting as if they exist. You've got the power to manifest what you want today and every day.

7. Give yourself the advice you'd give others.

SELF INVESTMENT STEPS

Take some time to list your triggers and create alternative ways of processing them. Your mood will change and lighten, and it will be of great benefit in managing your daily life, especially when these triggers next occur. Thinking about them in advance of them occurring will give you the pre-prepared thoughts and strategies for avoiding going down the auto-pilot rabbit hole of past negative behaviours.

In your Journal, make three columns. The heading of the first column is 'Trigger', the second is 'How it makes me feel', and the third is 'How I choose to feel'. Now, list your triggers and fill in columns 2 and 3. Here are some examples.

46

TRIGGER	HOW IT MAKES ME FEEL	HOW I CHOOSE TO FEEL
Bingeing	Disgusting	Forgiving, loving and compassionate – I have the power to change. I can talk to myself as I would to someone else who binges – with encouragement and support.
Body Image	Negative	Loving and kind – my body has faithfully supported me throughout my whole life.
Your job	Bored and frustrated	It's paying my bills and supporting my lifestyle. I can look for something else.
Colleagues	Annoyed	I may not be able to change someone, but I can change the way I feel about things. I choose to look for the positives in this situation.
Watching TV/Netflix etc	I always need a snack.	I'm keeping a food diary, and I'm also going to do gentle exercise from my sofa as I view. I can take up a hobby such as knitting, wordle, crocheting, or sudoku that I can do alongside watching a screen.

So take the time to contemplate your triggers and fill in the table as you wish.

Triggers Part 2

The second part of this chapter concerns my own experience of a couple of triggers that seemed to pop up out of nowhere and yet had probably been very powerfully sabotaging my efforts at getting my own habits and compulsions under control.

The unexpected triggers were Grief and Loss – I know it sounds bizarre, but I was subconsciously mourning for the loss of my bad habits!

What follows is how I dealt with my triggers in regard to alcohol, but it can equally apply to triggers one experiences with food compulsions, habits and addictions.

As I've said before, we've all got our triggers. I've devoted this chapter to them. However, recently, I discovered those two powerful and disruptive triggers that I didn't even know I had.

Like me, since you're reading this book, you may also have experienced addictive behaviours. Mine was not so much about food but centred around wine, and this led me to frequently eat unhealthily. I've known that I've had this book in me for years, but I was never able to write it because alcohol was a drain on me. It was both my friend and my enemy. Over the years, I tried to resist it, but I looked forward to it, even though I knew that as soon as I had my first sip of wine, it was like a valve had been opened, and all my creativity, commitment, focus and motivation drained away. This happened regularly, day after day, time after time over the years. It's not that I was a falling-over drunk, and no one would have suspected that I had a problem because, on the face of it, I'm a high-functioning, successful woman. But I knew I had a problem with addictive behaviour – because every time I tried to stop, I couldn't. Perhaps you can also relate to this mental state in regard to your relationship with food.

Just like you, I had all the beliefs and associated mindset that had built up over the years to give me the inner destructive language to support my bad habit. I had been drinking alcohol for 40 years! The chapters in this book have been inspired by my struggle over the years and how difficult I found it to change my thoughts and behaviours until I became so much more self-questioning and self-aware. This awakening was integral in how I was able to alter my belief system. The wisdom I'm sharing in this book is what changed my life.

I'd like to share some important insights that took me by surprise: Even though I'd conscientiously worked hard at successfully changing my mindset, had made very good progress and had been alcohol-free for a long time, it came as a shock to me one day to discover some very strong and very uncomfortable emotions that I wasn't expecting.

At first, I didn't know what they were - Let me put it in context:

I'd been flat-out writing this book – almost all my spare time was devoted to thinking about it, researching it, typing it, rehearsing the words out loud, and finding a professional recording studio to record the chapters and a videographer to film a promotional video. I'd been pushing past my comfortable boundaries – I'd gone way beyond my normal limits and made huge investments of my time and money so that my experiences could help other people.

My first experience of making a professional recording of my words was nerve-wracking and extremely stressful, even though it all went very well. After I'd finished, I had to walk home through town, and I passed many inviting bars and bistros. I felt very discombobulated because my historical beliefs and behaviours would have taken me straight into a bar to 'celebrate', to de-stress, to reflect on it all – to share it all with my 'best friend'. That 'best friend' being wine. My 'best friend' who had remained consistent, never let me down and was always there for me over the years, in good times and bad.

So it felt empty and strange that I wasn't going to a bar to meet my best friend. Very uncomfortable indeed, and I didn't recognise these disagreeable emotions. I felt that something was missing – I should be delighted that I had successfully recorded the first set of chapters, and I should be delighted that I hadn't touched alcohol in a long, long time, and yet I felt perplexed. When I contemplated my feelings, I realised that what I was experiencing was grief and loss! Grief at the loss of my 'best friend' – my faithful, constant companion who'd been with me through thick and thin. Alcohol wasn't ever doing me any favours, but it was familiar and had accompanied me through almost everything in my life since my mid-teens. I was in mourning. Adjusting to a missing element in my life.

Once I recognised what the emotions were, it all started to make sense as to why I felt so uncomfortable. Once I was able to label my emotions, I felt so much stronger and better able to deal with them. Acknowledging them seemed to release me from them and made me feel more in command of my thoughts and feelings. That realisation was my 'Get out of Jail free' card. It gave me a sense of peace, power, and self-compassion, and I was so much better equipped to go forward without succumbing to temptation.

So I'm sharing this with you because if you've also had a lifelong habit of dipping into the cookie jar to support you, then it's important that you also acknowledge that when you don't have this so-called 'support', you'll likely experience similar feelings of discombobulation.   However, as I discovered, recognising them, understanding them, accepting them, and applying a different sort of self-talk can see you through.

This leads me to a powerful 'Self-Talk' tool:

The Talking Out Loud Tool:

There was a day when I was driving in my car, and I suddenly felt absolutely wretched, overwhelmed with a sense of emotional discomfort. I felt tired and overwrought. I felt tearful. I felt triggered and I knew that previously, I would have sought refuge and comfort in wine, but I wasn't going to do that this time. I knew that I could sit with the uncomfortable feelings, and they'd eventually go away, but what I did was a faster technique: I started talking to myself out loud. It was so helpful and helped me to rationalise things so much quicker. When we experience negative emotions and don't do anything about them, then they can just loop around our minds over and over and may lead to self-sabotage. So here are two techniques to shift them:

1. As I've said, privately speak your thoughts out loud to yourself. Have a conversation with yourself. Respond to yourself in the 3rd person. I've previously mentioned that speaking our thoughts out loud slows them down and can very effectively rationalise them. Speaking to yourself in the car is often an ideal time for this. I also speak to myself when I go for walks. I speak to myself in the house. It may be that you're in a situation where you can't talk to yourself out loud, so before you act on any cravings or negative emotions, tell yourself that you're going to have a word with yourself later.

2. Speak your thoughts into your phone. I've mentioned journaling before and how useful it is to write things down, but sometimes it's more expedient and practical to speak your thoughts out loud. However, recording your thoughts on your phone gives you the tool to refer back to them at a later date. And record the good thoughts, too! There are also apps that can transcribe your audio to text so you can even read it later.

CHAPTER 10

MANAGING BOREDOM

Rewiring automatic behaviour.

Studies have shown that although many people emotionally eat when they experience feelings of stress, sadness, anger, frustration, etc, it's boredom that triggers emotional eating most of all!

Boredom can be a massive factor in unhealthy choices about our eating. When we're bored and unstimulated, reaching for the cookie jar can seem like the most obvious and attractive thing to do. But boredom eating provides little reward and can lead to long-term dissatisfaction, which can encourage you to eat even more and feel worse than you did.

So, how do you recognise the difference between real hunger and psychological hunger? Recognising this simple fact is key in controlling what we eat. Knowing the difference can help you know when to start applying the tips in this module's Self-Investment Steps section.

Actual hunger signs can be tummy rumbling, light-headedness, headache, sore tummy, and short-temperedness (hangry).

A way of recognising if you are actually hungry is to ask yourself if you would like any of a wide range of healthy food that you like – it could be superfoods, protein bars, yoghurt, fresh fruit, dried fruit .... Because if you are genuinely hungry, then some or all of these will appeal to you! Or is it a particular food item that you want, and only that food item will satisfy you – chocolate or biscuits, for example? If that is the case, then you most likely want to eat for reasons other than hunger.

In other words, it's something for you to do when there's nothing else to keep your mind occupied or stimulated. This may already have become your automatic behaviour.

However, you can restore emotional power to your food choices by rewiring your automatic behaviour.

SELF INVESTMENT STEPS – consider and apply all or some of the following:

Here are some suggestions for breaking patterns and re-wiring your thoughts and actions:

First of all, **CREATING PATTERNS.**

Your mind is constantly looking for patterns. Your mind looks for familiarity and repetition. By establishing healthy habits, your subconscious will support you by quickly embedding them, and it will become easier and easier for you to sustain these healthy routines.

- Plan ahead – schedule your day so that there aren't any large gaps.
- Plan your eating – create food windows for each meal, for example – Breakfast 7.00 am-9.00 am, Lunch 12 noon – 1.30 pm, Evening Meal 6.00 pm – 7.30 pm. It's a very good idea to mark these windows on your weekly planner.
- Plan your meals and snacks in advance.
- Plan when you're going to shop for them.
- Prepare nutritious snacks in advance – sliced red peppers, cucumber, carrot batons, frozen cherries …
- Make yourself a fitness regime for Mon-Fri. Break it up by resting at the weekend or doing a different one.
- Write a daily journal to record your thoughts.

CHANGING HABITS

Habits are part of our lives – recognise if they are serving you (for example, do you have a habit of grazing when you're relaxing in the evening) and, if you have a habit that's not serving you, break your pattern by trying something new instead. Here are some suggestions:

- Make a To Do list of things you require to accomplish and attack one of them when you're feeling bored (for example - decluttering, cleaning, sorting your inbox, making folders of your photographs, sorting your wardrobe).
- Brush your teeth – it's a distraction and can send signals to the brain that it's time to stop eating!
- Give yourself 5-10 minutes to write a list of what you're grateful for. Nothing is too small or too big. It will distract you. Make sure it's not just repetitive – stretch your mind to find new things! (For example, it's a sunny day, you've just accomplished a task, a book you're enjoying reading, a good conversation with someone close). It's a great distraction and a great mood booster!
- Listen to motivational and inspirational Podcasts or Talks on YouTube
- Invest in some fruit teas – the sweetness may be all you need to curb your cravings for sweetness while you are reprogramming your mindset.
- Learn a new skill: sewing, painting, handcraft, woodcraft, a foreign language …
- Write a short story – plan its structure/characters, etc. If it was made into a film, which actors would you cast in it.
- Make photo albums of pics on your phone/PC, etc.
- Make yourself a fitness regime for Mon-Fri. Break it up by resting at the weekend or doing a different one (I know I've already mentioned this in Creating Patterns)
- Broaden your mind – subscribe to the History Channel or Discovery Channel

- Stimulate those little grey cells by regularly doing Sudoku, Wordle, Quizzes, etc
- Perhaps you like colouring – invest in a colouring book. It's relaxing, therapeutic and you're doing something with your hands.
- Physiologically, we can experience a mid-afternoon dip – make sure you have something nutritious to eat if you need something – some seeds, a protein bar, fruit, etc.
- Write a daily journal to record your thoughts. (I know I've already mentioned this in Creating Patterns).
- Phone a friend/family member.
- Learn poetry.
- Play an online game with a friend – scrabble, chess. They don't even have to be in the same country!

AND THE 64 MILLION DOLLAR QUESTION IS..... DRUMROLL …

Now that you have read the above, what will YOU do TODAY??????

CHAPTER 11

SELF-TALK

It's our thoughts that create our success or failure.

The thoughts we put into our minds are far more important than the food we put into our mouths. It's our thoughts that dictate our success or failure. The messages and stories that we tell ourselves will either encourage, motivate and support us, or they will limit us because they are negative. These negative messages are usually what causes the self-sabotage syndrome of yo-yo dieting.

Let me explain the simple yet so powerful process by which our thoughts create our lives:
Our thoughts become words
Our words become our self-talk.
Our self-talk becomes our beliefs.
Our beliefs become our behaviours.
Our behaviours become our habits.
And our habits shape our lives.

How do you regularly talk to yourself?

Here's a simple exercise: Imagine a female friend comes to you and says she knows she's overweight, knows how to eat healthily, and knows what she should do to help herself lose weight. However, she regularly loses control and sabotages her weight loss attempts by bingeing on all the wrong sorts of food. So, instead of losing weight, she's gaining weight! She feels out of control and doesn't know how to stop. It makes her miserable, so she just eats more! (*By the way, does this sound familiar – is this actually your story?*)

So, how would you respond to your friend? Your words to your friend would likely be encouraging, supportive, kind and helpful. Because if you were to tell your friend that she's ugly and pathetic, that you're so disappointed in her, that you hate her body, that she is worthless and should just carry on bingeing, that she doesn't even deserve to succeed, this language would hurt your friend and diminish the relationship that you have with one another. The language would likely make your friend feel worse and even less inclined to feel she has what it takes to sustainably reduce her weight. It would be an attack on her self-esteem. *But is this actually what you secretly tell yourself?*

The language I've just described may be negative, but it's extremely powerful in reinforcing negative self-image and directing unhealthy choices about what we eat.

If that language is the secret inner dialogue you use towards yourself, then you can be setting yourself up for failure. It can be very difficult to break the low mood spiral that those toxic words encourage. It's the language of the inner critic. And the inner critic just masquerades as being helpful - most of us have the delusion that if we speak harsh words to ourselves, they will keep us on the right track. However, in actual fact, in my experience, it's the opposite of what we need to hear. Words are powerful weapons and can do massive damage. The sense of diminishment from these unpleasant words can severely affect our motivation.

The simple solution is to imagine that you are your best friend and talk to yourself with the same compassion, kindness, encouragement and support you would use towards your friend. In so doing, you can empower yourself and create sustainable positive change. One of the reasons I regularly talk out loud to myself is so that my subconscious mind can actually hear me speaking my words of self-encouragement and support. And hearing them out loud also buoys me up!

So stop right now and consider the words and language you use to describe yourself.

Are you under the delusion that creating an inner critic is going to positively empower you? Then think again - How long have you been battling with your weight? How long have you had that inner critic? Sounds to me like it's time to change.
Remember - Your thoughts become your outcomes!

SELF INVESTMENT STEPS

Speak to yourself like you're your own best friend!!!!
Words of encouragement, support, understanding, tolerance, patience, forgiveness, compassion, love, consideration and humour! Lighten up!

These are the words needed to create the best version of yourself. And keep at it! It may sound a bit odd initially to encourage yourself this way, but I promise you it works in changing failure into success.

In your private moments, speak the words out loud to yourself!
Physically pat yourself on the back!
Identify and celebrate any successes you have had!

If you feel weary, remember that:

Coca-Cola only sold 25 bottles in the first year!
James Dyson made 5,127 prototypes before getting it right!
Twelve publishers turned down J K Rowling!
Believe in your own success!

And here's an additional tool for reinforcement. I call it,

MIRROR MIRROR ON THE WALL ...

If you look in mirrors (not everyone does), each time you look into the mirror, say "Hello Beautiful!!!!" "Hi, Gorgeous!!" Either mentally or out loud. It may seem alien to begin with, but the mind learns through repetition. You may be aware that every time you look in the mirror or think about your body, you have negative thoughts. Well, these are exactly the thoughts that are keeping you stuck in your lack of success when it comes to healthily, successfully and sustainably reducing your weight. When you start to consciously think and speak positively to yourself, you are programming your subconscious and the subconscious will give you more of those feelgood feelings!!!

When you feel good about yourself you are so much more likely to reward yourself with positive choices regarding what you eat, where you eat, why you eat, when you eat, how you eat and how much you eat!

What are you waiting for?????? You have the power and you have all the tools you need!!!!

CHAPTER 12
PLAN AND PREP/NUTRITION

Here are ten ways to nurture your nutrition:

1. **Stay balanced:** In general, your meals should contain a good balance of protein, good carbs, colourful veggies and healthy fats.

2. **Start as you mean to go on:** If you like to eat three meals per day, make sure to eat a decent breakfast, like porridge and fruit, or eggs and wholemeal toast or something equally nutritious. That way, you won't be tempted by pastries later on – and the blood sugar spikes and drops they lead to. If you prefer to fast intermittently and eat only two main meals daily, the same guidelines apply.

3. **Pack some protein:** This is worth a point of its own, as many of us forget the importance of protein. Omitting it can lead to imbalances in blood sugar and pesky cravings – whereas including meat, fish, nuts, seeds, pulses, or tofu in every meal keeps these urges at bay.

4. **Choose healthy carbs:** They ARE NOT the enemy! Without them, our blood sugar becomes unstable – affecting our serotonin levels, our mood, and our sleep. So choose high-fibre, slow-releasing carbs like wholemeal grains, sweet potatoes, rolled oats, quinoa, brown rice, peas, pulses, lentils, nuts, nut butter, rye bread, and fruits.

5. **Find good fats:** Sources of healthy fats, like oily fish, avocados, olive oil, and nuts and seeds, reduce inflammation in the body. They also keep your heart healthy, skin clear, and hair strong. They're basically superheroes in your diet. So don't neglect them.

6. **Go with your gut:** Maintaining a healthy gut is essential for your immune system. Remember, the more diverse your diet, the more diverse your gut microbes are and the better your health. So enjoy a varied diet including prebiotics – that's fibre rich foods such as fruits, vegetables and whole grains, and probiotics which can be found in fermented foods like kimchi, sauerkraut, kefir and yoghurt, and keep your gut happy.

7. **Keep hydrated:** Drink plenty of water and other fluids because dehydration can lead to unhealthy food cravings.

8. **Enjoy sweet experiences, not sweet treats:** Replace your cravings for sugary snacks with the natural high of fun social activities. Whether it's enjoying a sunset, a lively conversation or your favourite hobby, set your intention to seek pleasure from healthier sources.

9. **Make friends with Magnesium:** Magnesium is something many of us are deficient in, which can impact our sugar levels, mood, and ability to handle cravings. You can pick up Magnesium supplements or sprays in your local health food store.

10. **Invest in a Fitness App:** Fitness apps allow users to track their progress and monitor their fitness goals. You can easily track meals, weight, workouts, blood pressure, heart rate, sleep, and other things. It allows you to see your progress and make any necessary adjustments to your fitness routine as needed.

SELF INVESTMENT STEPS

It's time for you to start planning.

- Does your diet need to change?
- What modifications do you need to make in order to make it more balanced and nutritious?
- What would you like to add?
- How can you create more variety?
- Where would you find healthy recipes?
- Is batch cooking an option for you?
- Soups and Smoothies are an amazing, versatile, healthy and inexpensive way to incorporate masses of good food into one thing.
- What's your budget?

Being prepared makes it so much easier to stay on track with healthy eating.

Think ahead and make a plan of what you are going to eat.

CHAPTER 13
SELF-REFLECTION

If we don't contemplate why we made unhealthy choices, we'll struggle to change our mindset and long-term behaviours.

CHECKING IN WITH YOURSELF AT THE END OF EACH DAY– I cannot overestimate how powerful this time of self-reflection is in creating your sustainable, healthy mindset.

Having a daily practice of contemplation is an essential part of your weight loss journey. It's an enjoyable discipline where you can learn more about yourself – acknowledging and celebrating your successes and acknowledging and considering what didn't go so well. If you don't spend time reflecting, you can miss out on a huge opportunity for self-discovery, self-awareness, and sustainable self-empowerment.

Now, not every day will go as we would have hoped – just as well as otherwise, if life was perfect, it would be boring - there would be no stimulus for change, growth and realising our potential!

To be honest - some days, we make decisions and choices about food or other things that we'd rather we hadn't, and we can beat ourselves up about that and keep replaying the script in our mind over and over. However, if we leave it at the head-bashing, then we're denying ourselves the opportunity to learn more about ourselves. What I'm about to reiterate is really, really, really important:

If we don't reflect on the reasons why we made certain choices and then contemplate them, we'll struggle to change our mindset and long-term behaviours.

Many people find that their own daily personal, private space where they can take time to themselves and reflect is the most valuable part of their day. This isn't meditation, and it's not prayer – it's about consciously drilling down deep and questioning ourselves - holding ourselves accountable for the repetitive thoughts and behaviours that have kept us stuck in negative patterns and cycles in our lives.

SELF INVESTMENT STEPS

Experiment regarding when would be the best time of your day to fit this time of reflection into your daily routine – it has to be a practical and comfortable time and a time when you are least likely to be disturbed.
It could be on your commute home, when you're in bed, or some other time that works well for you. The easier you make this time, the more likely you are to do it!

Make sure you have your journal – whether that's a written one or an electronic one.

So here are four suggestions to consider:
- What went well today?
- What could have gone better today?
- What can I learn from today and change going forward?
- What are my action steps – mentally and physically?

As I mentioned earlier, I cannot overestimate how powerful this time of self-reflection is in creating your sustainable, healthy mindset.

And enjoy it!

Make a point of enjoying this process – it's an important investment in YOUR WELLBEING!!!!

CHAPTER 14

INTERMITTENT FASTING

It's less about resisting foods but choosing and committing to times when you simply don't eat food.

Intermittent fasting works by prolonging the period when your body has burned through the calories consumed during your last meal and begins burning fat.

Additionally, because our bodies conserve energy during fasting, our basal metabolic rate (the amount of energy our bodies burn while resting) becomes more efficient, lowering our heart rate and blood pressure and burning calories.

It's about having set windows when you know you will be eating (healthily) and set periods when you will not be eating at all - you can still drink – it's important to stay hydrated.

It gives the digestive system a long period of time to rest and rejuvenate.
It's not for everyone, though – and there are some medical conditions where it is not recommended, so if it appeals to you, please thoroughly check it out and get plenty of information on it or talk to your health care professional.

However, I include it here as a chapter as it is very helpful for a lot of people: Knowing exactly when you can and can't eat takes that sense of indecision and uncertainty out of things. It's not so much about resisting foods but choosing and committing to times when you simply don't eat food. And it can provide significant health benefits, including, of course, weight loss.

Recently, it has become more and more popular and is recognised as a healthy and sustainable life choice for losing weight. Please note that I said "sustainable life choice for losing weight" rather than the word diet!!!! (that's a little reminder from a previous chapter). You can incorporate it into your life by fasting from dinner until you break your fast the next day – making it part of your healthy everyday life!

SELF INVESTMENT STEPS

As I mentioned above, if you feel that Intermittent Fasting appeals to you, then make sure you research it. There's loads of information online. There are also books and podcasts, etc. However, it's very wise to run it past your healthcare professional if you want to check out any pre-existing conditions that would mean Intermittent Fasting wouldn't suit you.
If you do feel that you would like to try it, then think about your lifestyle – your daily routines and what would work for you. There are a number of methods, and I'll mention two here:

Daily Time Restricted Eating is a form of Intermittent Fasting:

The 12/12 method is often a technique used by many people – they have a 12-hour eating window from, say, 7 am – 7 pm for their 2 or 3 meals per day, and then they fast from food from 7 pm – 7 am.

In my experience, most people have two healthy main meals and a snack mid-afternoon to sustain them.

Some of my clients prefer to eat between 11 am – 7 pm. They enjoy a brunch and then a fairly early dinner. And a healthy snack in between. So their fasting period is between 7 pm and 11 am – that's 16 hours.

Another type of Intermittent Fasting is the 5:2 method.

The 5:2 method is a fasting regime in which the calorie intake is limited twice a week to 500-600 calories per day, with more normal healthy eating on the other five days.

Because there are no requirements about what foods you can or can't eat, but rather when you should eat them, this method is more of a lifestyle, and you can incorporate your healthy food choices around it. You can plan your meals for the five days and eat normally while still being conscious of your calorie intake.

And the types of foods which you can eat on the fast days can include:

A generous portion of vegetables, natural yoghurt with berries, boiled or baked eggs, grilled fish or lean meat, cauliflower rice, soups, black tea and coffee.

So, I've outlined two methods, but there are many others. I recommend that you do some research, think about what would work for you, and, very importantly, enjoy the ride!

CHAPTER 15
EATING YOUR GREENS

Eating the Rainbow and Eating the Alphabet!

Did you know that your happy hormones are created in the gut?

Your gut health has a strong influence on your mood. We produce the hormone 'serotonin' in our gut, which is a 'feel-good chemical' that directly affects our feelings. Serotonin is a neurotransmitter – a messenger that relays information between different parts of the brain and nervous system. It also directly affects our sleep cycles because the brain uses it to make melatonin – a hormone that regulates sleep.

Your gut manufactures up to 95% of your body's serotonin, and a healthy serotonin level in the gut helps you feel calmer, happier, more focused, and less stressed. In addition, a healthy level of serotonin also boosts your immune system, reduces inflammation, helps to maintain a healthy weight, increases fibre and can even lower cancer risks. Plant-based foods are generally high in serotonin. Plants have essential nutrients that you cannot get from other foods. The natural vitamins and minerals in plants help keep your cells healthy and your body balanced so that you can function at your best.

YOU have the power to improve the way you feel by controlling what you put on your plate. So, I recommend deliberately using that power to enhance your mood and lifestyle. Eating more greens and plant-based foods can support you in this.

Let's start by looking at Salads

Eating salads and vegetables before eating the rest of the food on your plate is an easy and healthy way of filling up with nutritious, low-calorie food.

Salads are full of volume and take time to cut and crunch, and they are quite hard to eat quickly, so this allows us to tune into our fullness signals. Research shows that beginning a meal with a green salad leads us to consume fewer calories over a meal. When I was young, a salad consisted of lettuce, cucumber and tomato! This no longer has to be the case – salads can be so interesting and nutritious. There are so many different salad offerings in shops and supermarkets, including seeds, nuts, grains, pulses, spices and dressings! I also include fruits with my salads. I make a tasty salad with strawberries, feta cheese, avocado and pecans. It's a fun and colourful way to combine health benefits with weight loss!!

Vegetables

The same applies to vegetables – I used to associate vegetables with simply being boiled – cabbage, broccoli, carrots! It kind of put me off them for a number of years! But so many more vegetables are available to us now (kale and okra are 2 of my favourites). Even sea vegetables are readily available now – kelp, dulse, spirulina – all packed full of goodness. And so many easy-to-access recipes online provide interesting cooking methods - steaming, roasting, baking vegetables, often combining them with interesting spices or herbs.

Smoothies

Smoothies are a convenient, delicious, versatile and healthy way to get a variety of vitamins and nutrients into your diet. They're essentially just a blended mixture of fruits, vegetables, liquid, and sometimes other ingredients such as nuts, seeds, oats, yoghurt and ice. They can help to promote digestive health, boost energy and brain function, support weight management, and are versatile and customisable to suit individual preferences. You can even add protein powder to them to get an easy extra nutrition boost without spending time preparing meals. They're nutritious, easy to make, filling and can help you lose weight without skipping meals.

I appreciate that some people have digestive ailments, and I recommend that they simply experiment with what works best for them!

SELF-INVESTMENT STEPS - Eating the Alphabet!

Most of us have heard about Eating the Rainbow - various coloured foods on your plate – but have you considered Eating the Alphabet?

Many people think that they eat a healthy amount of salad/fruit/veg, but when they actually make a list of the varieties they eat, they tend to find that they're eating the same ones week in and week out – often up to a maximum of about 6. Have a think just now and count up the different types of veggies and fruit you eat each week. Are they quite repetitive? As I mentioned, our gut health directly impacts our well-being and happiness as serotonin – the happy hormone – is created in the gut. So it's essential to keep our gut microflora –the healthy bacteria in our gut – as healthy as possible with a varied diet.

Plan on "Eating the Rainbow" each day – a varied selection of different coloured vegetables & salads on your plate. However, if you want to consider easily extending your range of plant-based foods and bringing more variety into your diet, you can access my "Eating the Alphabet' document, which you can download from my website at www.changewithgillian.com/bookresources/

This gives you an alphabetical list of different plant-based foods that you may not have considered.

Have fun with it – why not eat your name!!! My name is Gillian – G – green beans, ginger, garlic, I – Iceberg Lettuce, L – Leeks, Lentils, L- Leaves, Lemon Grass, I -Indian Figs, N – Nigella Seeds, Nectarines, Nuts.

Have fun!!! Enjoy it!!!!!!!

Make a list of the foods you would like to try. Experiment with them, as I say, have fun! It's a journey and a healthy eating food adventure!!! This is all feeding into your emotional and physical well-being – the better you feel, the more likely you are to make sustainable, healthy choices. This is all part of celebrating you!!!!

CHAPTER 16

ARE YOU HUNGRY OR THIRSTY?

A very important question to ask yourself.

Many of us simply don't drink enough water. As a result, we can get our signals confused and think we're hungry when we are actually thirsty! It's a form of unconscious self-neglect. We've got into the habit of stretching towards the cookie jar, thinking that is what we need and that's what's going to satisfy a craving, without realising that we actually need more hydration! Stop here and reflect – is that YOU?

We often simply don't drink enough water throughout the day. Water – is the elixir of life, and it has no calories! Water increases our energy, giving us better concentration, positivity and overall health. It also helps with digestion because it aids our ability to flush out toxins.

I've helped thousands of people with their weight loss endeavours, and it's a recurring theme that many people simply don't drink enough water. The thing is, they often know this, but they still don't do anything about it!

SELF INVESTMENT STEPS

Everyone is different, but it's recommended that we have at least around 1.5 litres of water each day (that's around two and a half pints). It could be straight water, herbal or fruit teas. But it's a good idea to have a way of measuring it – get yourself a transparent water bottle and keep it near you. That way, you can gauge throughout the day how much you have drunk and if you need to drink more. Aim to fill it up in the morning, refill it at lunchtime, and refill it early in the evening! If you feel that evening drinking disrupts your sleep, just drink more during the day if this suits you.

Some people put an alarm on their phone to remind them it's time to drink.

Another tip is to buy a big 2-litre bottle of water and keep it in your kitchen or workspace. Commit to drinking it by the end of the day. You might drink it as straight water or use it in your tea, but by keeping this around you, you have a daily monitor regarding how much water you have consumed and a reminder if you haven't drunk enough. You don't have to buy a new one each day; you can just keep refilling it daily.

Water can be consumed instead of sweetened juices and sodas. You can flavour your water naturally by adding fresh mint, sliced cucumber, lemon or lime.

Drinking water before a meal can also help prevent overeating by creating a sense of fullness.

Water helps us to break down food and aids in digestion and the elimination of waste.
Have a think about whether you need to increase your daily water intake, and if so, how you're going to do it.

Now, here's another of my **Mind Magic Moments**:

We know that around 70% of our body is water.

However, did you know that it's been scientifically proven that water holds memories? (Research by the Resonance Science Foundation). In addition, a Japanese doctor – Dr Masaru Emoto, discovered through his research that the molecules in water are affected by our thoughts, words and feelings. How amazing is that????

So, to my mind, it's logical that we can programme the water we drink by simply directing our thoughts to the water before we drink it - and lovingly asking that the water be blessed and that it refreshes us and gives us optimum health and energy.

You may think I'm bonkers, but I know that the water I drink each time I do this tastes better and makes me feel better, too!

Try it and see – what have you got to lose?

CHAPTER 17

THE SCALES

Consider NOT handing over your daily emotional well-being and control to a number.

When we are in the process of reducing our weight, it can seem very motivating to track our progress on the scales. However, sometimes, this can be a double-edged sword, and if it intrinsically affects our emotional state when we see a number on the scales that disappoints us, then this can be very dangerous territory.

We must understand that the scales are not the be-all-and-end-all measure of our success or failure – they are simply an indicator of our weight loss journey.

To illustrate my point, here are three typical scenarios I've encountered from clients who have been actively trying to lose weight:

RESULT A – Person steps on the scales – **NO WEIGHT REDUCTION**

Their THOUGHTS: I've been good all week – I thought I would have lost weight.
Their FEELINGS: – disillusioned, this just isn't working. I should have known better.
I can't do this. What's the point?

Possible OUTCOME: I'm giving up, and I'm just going to eat junk because that gives me comfort. I'll start again next Monday. (Secret thinking – thank goodness I've got an excuse to get off this diet!)

RESULT B – Person steps on the scales – **NOT MUCH WEIGHT REDUCTION**

Their THOUGHTS: – Disappointing - I was hoping to have lost more. However, I have a choice here. I'm at a fork in the road: I can feel disillusioned and just give up, or I can stay optimistic because at least I've lost something.

Their FEELINGS: – There's still hope and opportunity to lose weight.
Possible OUTCOME: Their motivation is diminished, so it can go either way - Give it more time or give it up.

RESULT C – Person steps on the scales – **LOST WEIGHT**
Their THOUGHTS: OH WOW!!!! This is fantastic and the motivation to continue my healthy weight loss plan.

Possible OUTCOME: they continue on the journey
OR, they have Dangerous THOUGHTS - Ooh, Fab! I've lost weight! I can afford a treat.
OUTCOME – less weight loss, possible sabotage, disappointment the next time they step on the scales, often leading to the usual repetitive failure cycle!

These examples show the fine line we tread between success and sabotage when we step on the scales. How fragile our equilibrium is. How destabilising the number we see on the scales can be. How often has the number you've seen on the scales disappointed you and thrown you off track?

SELF INVESTMENT STEPS

Basically, there can be so many reasons attributed to our weight loss – what we eat and drink, how much salt we consume, how much exercise we have done, how we're feeling, the time of the month, even the cycles of the moon can affect our weight loss.

When we're in the process of weight reduction, it seems to me that to hand over the power of what we are doing for ourselves to an external object like a pair of scales in order to evaluate our progress and set our emotional well-being for the day, can be exceptionally destabilising.

So, in light of what I have just said, consider very carefully what part weighing yourself has played in the success and failures of your weight journey. Did weighing yourself really give you control? If so, why are you still battling the lbs? Have you been weighing yourself too often? I'm not saying to chuck your scales out, but I am saying that you should prepare yourself mentally BEFORE you stand on the scales.

I had a client who came to work with me because she had been attending weight loss clubs for 30 years, and although she lost weight at different periods in her life, she had progressively gotten heavier and heavier over the years. She told me she weighed herself every day. I asked her why. She told me that it gave her control! I asked her (tactfully) how she could consider that weighing herself daily was giving her control when her experience was that, over the last 30 years, she had progressively kept gaining weight. She had never thought of this before! It certainly gave her food for thought (pardon the pun!). She realised she was giving away her power and control to the figure she saw on the scales daily, and this wasn't supporting her. She took my advice and put her scales in the garage and only weighed herself once every two weeks. Although initially, she found not weighing herself every day hard, it soon gave her a sense of freedom and release. She became more aware of her feelings and emotions and how the positive feelings and suggestions I'm about to describe to you could sustainably support her mental well-being and weight loss intentions so much more.

Before you get on the scales, it's really important to take the time to set your mindset so you're less emotionally affected by whatever number you see on the scales.

Commit time to consider things about yourself, such as:

- I've been eating better, and I feel less bloat.
- My energy has increased.
- I've been moving/exercising more – that makes me feel good and proud.
- What positive changes can I notice now that I've altered my eating habits?
- What makes me feel good about myself?
- What are my achievements?
- What qualities do I possess that make me proud? It can be as simple as recognising that you're a good friend, parent, or effective worker, feeling virtuous because you cleaned your home, learned a new skill, finished a course of study, bought someone a gift you know they'll love, gave to the food bank, called someone you hadn't spoken to in too long ....

Choose whatever works for you, but it's the positive attitude of mind this gives you that expands your thinking and helps to prevent you from dropping down the rabbit hole of despair if you see a number on the scales that disappoints you. It keeps your vibration high and helps you to be more philosophical about the journey and not stuck in the moment.

Lastly, have a think and commit to weighing yourself less regularly – perhaps even just once or twice a month. Try it and see how it makes you feel.

CHAPTER 18

SLEEP

Sleep deprivation has been linked to poor food choices.

You might wonder what sleep has to do with craving sugar, but lack of sleep is a key reason you may want to eat something sweet! Your hunger hormones, ghrelin and leptin, are affected by your sleep, so ensure you get optimum sleep during the night. A good night's sleep is affected by what you do during the day. Here are your

SELF INVESTMENT STEPS

1.	Get outside – get at least 20 minutes of fresh air and natural light every day as early as possible in the morning. Your body thrives on natural light, and studies have shown that good sleep is connected with exposure to daylight as early as possible in the morning.
	However, if you can't make it in the morning – make it any time of the day.

	Have a conscious awareness and intention that the simple act of being outside is having a dynamic effect on your sleep and sleep quality. Set your intention that you're going to have an even better sleep tonight because you've been outside today and been enjoying the elements – whatever the weather. Use all your senses to enjoy it – consider what you can feel, see, hear, smell, taste and touch. Really immerse yourself in the experience of simply being outside. We generally don't consciously use our senses enough. Be in the moment.

2. Stop drinking caffeine by noon – or better still, stop drinking caffeine full stop!
3. Stop eating 2 – 3 hours before bed.
4. Stop looking at screens 1 hour before bed – if you absolutely HAVE to look at a screen, then use Blue Light blocking glasses – these reduce the glare from a screen, which prohibits the production of melatonin – the hormone associated with the control of sleep.
5. Give your body sleep signals – consistent regular indicators that you're winding down for the day – and keep to a pattern. Use discipline. You're programming your mind in this way.

   Have a bedtime ritual – at the same time each evening, start getting yourself ready for bed - it could be a bit of stretching or yoga, a bath or shower, rhythmic breathing – in for 4, hold for 4, out for 6, empty for 4 – or whatever numbers work for you, journaling, checking in with yourself – see Chapter 13, listening to music, reading, counting your blessings …
6. Finally, simply set your intention for a good night's sleep – setting your intention is a powerful activator which is frequently ignored – simply decide that you are going to have a good night's sleep.

CHAPTER 19
MANAGING YOUR CRAVINGS

A craving is a feeling that can be preserved and strengthened by thoughts of trying to push it away! What you resist persists!

Cravings - We all have them occasionally, and conscious or unconscious triggers prompt them. Cravings are not the same as hunger, though, so if you decide to pass on them, they'll likely just go away!

However, recognising the triggers is a very important place to start.
There are various types of triggers:

I'm going to address three here - Social Triggers, Pattern Triggers and Emotional Triggers.

Social Triggers – You're in a situation where there is a lot of food – something social or a work event, and you would have previously dug into the goodies on offer. (BTW - NEVER go to these events hungry!)

Pattern Triggers revolve around habits you've become accustomed to within your day. For example, a sweet treat mid-afternoon, eating in the evening in front of a screen, eating snacks at the cinema, and having salty snacks with alcohol.

Emotional Triggers occur when we're faced with an emotional situation that we previously handled by stress, comfort or reward eating. This can also include the emotions of anger and frustration that we sometimes experience if we deny ourselves certain foods, such as chocolate, etc., and tell ourselves, "How come other people can eat chocolate and I can't?"

SELF INVESTMENT STEPS

So, let's get straight onto the Self-Investment Steps -
Here are a variety of techniques to help you manage cravings – you can consider which ones will help you best and at which times:

However, the first thing to consider is Self-Awareness:

What's really important with the steps is that we ACKNOWLEDGE the craving rather than try to push it away because trying to push it away or beating yourself up about having it will only make it worse.

Be aware that a craving is a feeling that's preserved and strengthened by your thoughts:
Very likely, your thoughts can be making the craving even worse! It's, therefore, very important to pay attention to your thoughts about it and the language you use towards it.

If you're having thoughts like "I'm not able to resist this urge", "I'm stuck with this craving", "I'm not strong enough to resist acting on this craving", "This craving just won't go away", then know this - these thoughts are strengthening the craving and increasing the intensity of the negative stress around it. (By the way, you may wish to refer back to Chapter 6 regarding the power of our words).

It may seem unbelievable, but you're ALWAYS in control of your thoughts, even in the middle of an intense craving.

So, first of all, rather than trying to resist the craving, start diminishing all the stress hormones you've been activating by trying to resist it, by instead acknowledging it, accepting the craving as part of a normal process, and telling yourself that the craving will pass. This lessens the resistance, relieves stress and helps the mind and body to relax.

Those stress hormones keep us stuck in the moment and make us more likely to act on unwanted behaviours.

Then question the thoughts – where have they come from? Think about the three types of triggers I've already mentioned. Get some rational thoughts on board, and you can also consider one or more of the steps I'm suggesting:

1. Being your own best friend:

I find it really helpful to have a conversation with myself in the 3rd person. I talk out loud to myself when I can because it slows down my thoughts and helps me see things more rationally. And I talk to myself as if I'm my best friend – words of support and encouragement – the same language that I would use to talk to someone if they were experiencing a craving. It helps to take me out of myself and diminish my negative thoughts and cravings.

2. Playing the tape forward:

When a craving occurs, our minds can instantly jump to how good it would be to eat that chocolate/cake/crisps/whatever … and in the past, you may have let your mind stay in that place. Quickly, the craving starts to strengthen and get to the irresistible stage.

With this technique - very importantly - you accept the craving and then think it forward.

What would happen if you had the 'treat'?
How soon would you start to experience negative feelings about yourself?
What would they make you do?
What would the outcome be?
How hard would it be to regain your control – would it be another binge week with the idea that you'd restart this coming Monday?
How many times have you been there before?

You may find it helpful to say these things out loud to yourself (as I mentioned previously – it will slow down your thoughts), or you could write them down – which will slow down your thoughts even more. Plus, you've got something to refer to the next time a pesky craving occurs.
(I'm a great advocator of the power of journaling).

Alternatively, with this technique, when you recognise the craving, you can choose to remember a time when you didn't succumb to the temptation –
What were your thoughts?
What happened?
What did you do instead?
Try to remember why you didn't act on the craving.

Re-acquaint yourself with those happy thoughts, as this will help to reprogram and emotionally strengthen you when cravings occur.

My personal tip – we may not always have our Journal to hand, but we do tend to have our phones 24/7. So I either record in the Notes section of my phone or on my 'Record and Transcribe' app under the heading "When I Triumphed!"
These are times when I recognised that I had a craving and resisted. I note down the day, date, time, what was happening, who I was with, what I did instead, and how I felt.
So if I experience a craving, I can readily access my notes, and by re-listening or re-reading them, it helps me to feel inspired – if I resisted before, I can do it again!!!!

If possible, I also take the time to journal the craving as I'm experiencing it – because, as I keep saying - getting out of your head and writing or typing it slows down your thoughts and starts to make the craving far more manageable.

3. Breathe
There is no such thing as 'breathing doesn't work for me!'

Deep, slow breathing oxygenates our blood, slows our heart rate, lowers blood pressure, promotes relaxation, reduces stress and – very importantly - alters our thoughts.

So get purposeful in changing your state of mind when a craving occurs:

Firstly, assess how strong the craving is on a scale of 0-10. (Zero – no craving).
– Sit down, if you can, look at a clock with a second hand or your phone's stopwatch and give yourself at least 2-3 minutes to breathe differently (I prefer 5 minutes).

Take stock of how you're feeling, set your intention for how you intend to feel after you've completed the breathing exercise, and then do a lovely, slow breathing technique.

My favourite is box breathing – In for 4, hold for 4, out for 6, empty for 4. (Nobody even has to know that you're doing it!). If you feel at all light-headed, then stop.

After a few minutes, take stock of how you're feeling now. Go back to your 0-10 scale.
Where are you on the scale now? If the craving hasn't already gone or significantly diminished where you won't act on it, do the breathing exercise again!

4. **The ABC Technique** *A - Activating Event, B - Beliefs, C - Consequences*
You're experiencing a craving – accept it and analyse it!
*What is the **A**ctivating Event* – the trigger - what brought it on?
***B**eliefs* – what irrational thoughts are you having about the craving?

For example:
1. It's going to last until I give in
2. It's overwhelming me
3. I have to give in to stop the craving

85

*C*onsequences – what are the emotional and behavioural results of the irrational beliefs?

1. Self-sabotage
2. Repetition of negative patterns

Then, dispute the irrational beliefs and replace them.

For example :

The Irrational belief:
"It's going to last until I give in" becomes "I know the craving will pass. Cravings have gone away in the past."
"It's overwhelming me" = "I'm strong enough to manage. I've managed before."
"I have to give in to stop the craving" = "I've successfully resisted before."
Consider other positive beliefs, such as
"I can find alternative distractions."
"I have the strength to counter the craving."
"Eating cake/pizza/crisps/chocolate won't fix the problem."
"Eating cake/pizza/crisps/chocolate makes things worse long term."
Return to your original irrational 'Beliefs" – are they still true?
Consider the original trigger – what is your response to it now?

5 The Timer Technique

When you experience a craving, set a timer (you could use your phone or a kitchen timer) for the length of time you're confident that you can withstand the experience of the craving – say, 3-5 minutes. Before you start the timer, decide what sort of activity you're going to do during the 3-5 minutes. Put the timer on and start the activity. When the timer sounds, there's a good chance that the craving will be weaker and less of a problem. At that point, you can decide if you want to reset the timer and repeat it or even reset the timer and do another activity. Alter the length of time on the timer to suit yourself.

As you get experience with this technique, you can set the timer for longer and longer periods. At some point, you may have set the timer for 20 or 30 minutes, and when the timer goes off, you realise that you'd forgotten that you'd put it on as you're so immersed in your activity.

This technique refocuses our mind. The more we do this, the more we train our minds to disregard the cravings.

6   *The Three Smiles technique*

This technique diminishes stress. In my experience, it's impossible to feel stress while practising this method.

1. Smile!
2. Take the happy energy of your smile down to your heart and imagine that your heart is also smiling!
3. Take the energy down further to a point in your belly behind your navel and about 5 cm (2 inches) lower. This is known as your Dantian point. It houses your vital energy, power and essence. Imagine that that part of your belly is also smiling.

Be aware of all three smiles simultaneously – you're smiling with your heart, body and mind, and just be still and breathe.

Be in this moment for as long as you can.

Experience the joy!

7   *Random quick craving crushers*

- Don't get hungry – eat regularly
- Have a large glass of water
- Take a walk or move to a different room
- Do a breathing exercise
- Call someone
- If there's a 'goody table' at work, suggest that the 'goodies' get put in a cabinet or drawer where they're not on show 24/7
- Take up a mind exercise like Sudoko, Wordle, Candy Crush or something similar
- Regularly listen to my meditation

- Make a list of your successes in life
- Make a list of your star qualities
- Make a list of things you're proud of
- Create positive affirmations
- Read your gratitude journal

CHAPTER 20

INTENTION SETTING

Language is a powerful tool in our sustainable success or failure.

Over the years, you've probably said sentences to yourself things like:

"I want to lose weight."
"I wish I could lose more weight."
"I hope I can stay on this diet."
"I've lost weight. I hope I can keep it off."

And since you're reading this book, those likely wants, wishes, and hopes didn't come true. Part of the reason for the failure is because these sentences are based on previous negative experiences - You haven't been successful in the past, and the subliminal message in these statements is to expect more of the same. The sentences hold an unconscious implication of failure - invisible messages that your subconscious picks up. All these sentences are infused with doubt and lack of personal power - for example - they could all be followed by the word 'but' …

"I want to lose weight, BUT *I've been unsuccessful in the past."* What follows the 'but' is the hidden meaning in the first part of the statement.

"I wish I could lose more weight, BUT *it'll likely be too hard"* – is the hidden message.

"I hope I can stay on this diet, BUT *I usually sabotage it after a while"* – again, what follows the 'but' is the unconscious message.

"I've lost weight, I hope I can keep it off, BUT, *it's unlikely*" – yet again, the statement has a latent implication.

In Chapter 6, I mentioned how the language we use is a powerful tool in our success or failure, and in this chapter, I'm making you aware of the potency of the language of desire and intent. In short, intention setting.

Once you're very clear on what you desire, for example, 'Losing X amount of weight in X amount of time', you can set this as your intention. An intention is not about "I want to lose weight; I hope I can make my goals; I hope I'm successfully able to lose the weight; I want to be able to stay on my diet." – these desires are all full of doubt.

Intention setting is a belief that even though you haven't yet achieved your goal, you're on your way. It's your internal GPS directing you and supporting you with the right information and beliefs that you're in the process of successfully achieving your goals.

Let me give you an analogy: I was recently invited to lunch in a village 20 miles away from where I live, and I'd never been there before. I didn't know where I was going, and I was expected to arrive by 12.30 pm. So, after looking at a map to show me the location, I was able to judge how long my journey would take. I set my GPS and set out in good time. I was able to follow a combination of what the GPS was telling me and road signs – the road signs being external markers and signals on my journey to support my belief that I was heading in the right direction. I'd set my intention to arrive on time, I had a clear idea of where I was going, and I had a realistic time frame and full belief that I was going to reach my destination accurately, safely and on time – which I did. I'd set my intention – a very clear intention, and I'd had clear markers along the way that I was going in the right direction. It could have happened that I took a wrong turn – but that wouldn't have meant that I'd need to go home and start all over again or abandon my journey. I would just have paused and re-routed! Such is the mind's attitude of intention. It gives us resolve and a firm determination that we are committed to achieving our goals.

Intentions are the mindset of decision, belief, positive expectation and positive outcome. And they give us the confidence that any unexpected 'bumps in the road' may result in a possible re-routing, but not an abandonment of our journey. Intentions are about realising that we don't need to leave things to chance - we're the script-writer, director, producer and leading actors in our lives, and we can control our outcomes. This belief enables us to harness our personal power and be so much more proactive in our lives by purposely choosing how we want to live it and the results we expect.

Clear intentions make us so much more likely to achieve our goals. Goals can feel very future-oriented and far away, but when we set a defined path with markers along the way and furnish it with daily re-affirming of our intentions, it can give us a sense of self-mastery, achievement and satisfaction as we progress towards our goal.

Once you've defined your goals, intention setting becomes the first step to achieving them and is a powerful tool for positively moving forward. Regularly stating and/or redefining your intention also helps to keep us on track and can even help us to quickly recognise when the path to the goal needs to change or, indeed if the actual goal needs to change. It can become clear very quickly when our intentions no longer align with the desired target.

So, those doubtful statements of

"I want to lose weight; "I wish I could lose more weight; "I hope I can stay on this diet; "I've lost weight, I hope I can keep it off."

Can now become more focused and purposeful statements that express a sense of ownership and confidence in the outcome. Such as:
"It is my intention that I'm able to healthily reduce my weight and keep it off."

There is a symbiotic relationship - a complex 2-way relationship - regarding the words you use, how they influence your subconscious mind, and how your subconscious will in return powerfully infuse your mind with those intents. And the more you repeat the intentions, the more they programme and code your subconscious mind and your belief system.

SELF INVESTMENT STEP

So, how do we set effective intentions:

- Clearly define your goal and realistic time frame
- Keep your language positive and in the present tense
- Using the words, "I am ..." gives your subconscious mind a clear message of commitment and ownership
- Repeat it daily. More often is even better
- Intentions can be modified or changed depending on your life's journey
- As you state your intention, experience the joy of having already achieved it!

So your intention could be, "I am in the process of healthily and sustainably achieving my ideal weight and shape by – add in a particular date. "

Intentions are the fuel to manifesting our goals and visions. Intentions create our realities.

CHAPTER 21
ACCOUNTABILITY

Keeping yourself accountable is a key factor in supporting yourself to achieve your weight loss goals.

Accountability plays a crucial role in keeping us on track. I'm outlining here various methods that you can use to develop your sense of motivation and accountability.

1. Journal

Sometimes, it's enough just to be accountable to oneself, so I'm emphasising the importance of keeping up with the journaling that I've been recommending in the book.
Keep referring to your journal to reinforce those important WHYS and WHY NOTS – it gives you clarity and helps to increase your focus and motivation.

Make your journal your best friend – whether it's a notebook, electronic, or both - prioritise its place in your life – your journal is your private space where you are recording your significant truths - and keep a daily or regular log of changes you are noticing.

Here's a suggested checklist that you can use. You can add to it if you wish.

- Energy – have you noticed a change and increase in your energy
- Less bloating
- Improvement in your productivity and motivation
- Improvement in self-esteem
- Improvement in self-confidence
- Drinking more water

- Enjoying food more – a sense of nourishment and nurturing yourself
- Looking after yourself better – facials, foot spa, manicure, massage
- Reading more and differently, listening to podcasts, talks on YouTube
- Exercising more
- Experiencing more peace of mind
- Decluttering
- Waking up happy with excitement for the day to come
- Improved sleep
- Feelings of pride

Also, record your daily thoughts – these can be very inspiring to reflect on.
And don't forget to include your wins!

2. A Mood Gamechanger: Counting Your Blessings.

In a previous chapter, I mentioned 'Counting your Blessings' and a Gratitude Journal. Well, in your Journal, at the end of the day, it really is a great idea to record at least three things that you feel grateful for that day. Try to make them different every day. It stretches your mind because sometimes it's not that easy to find three new things – sometimes it is easy, and you can list even more than 3 – but the premise of this exercise is that it wraps your mind around lots of positive things that you've experienced that day and by writing them down (even if it's just one word to remind you), you won't forget them.

This is a fantastic tool for lifting your mood when you may be feeling low or tempted by something because I promise you this: when you go back and re-read the things you've written, much of which you would have forgotten if you hadn't got them out of your head and into black and white, it is such a game-changer for your mood. It raises your spirits, alters your point of view and gives you a positive, fresh perspective on what you're doing and all the benefits it's been giving you. This is also another way of countering cravings.

Don't just leave it to chance that you'll remember positive and happy things; write them down, record them for posterity and then revisit them for a pick-me-up, especially when feeling low.

3. Weight Loss Apps
Numerous weight loss apps can help you measure your success and keep yourself accountable in various ways. They're not for everyone, but at least invest in yourself by looking at and exploring the various ways they can support you.

4. Food Diary or using an App
Some people find recording everything they eat during the day and the calories very useful. It can be done in a journal or electronically. Or, as I mentioned in the previous point, if you look online, you'll also find plenty of apps that can support you with this. Or you could consider investing in a FitBit-type app. These apps measure a whole range of things, from weight, food, fitness, sleep, heart rate and much more.

5. Accountability Partner
Perhaps you have someone with whom you can share your intended eating and exercise plans. Someone you can check in with regularly and discuss your success, your challenges, what's been working, and what you've been finding difficult. Having this share can help you keep on track. Your accountability partner could even take your measurements once a month. Your accountability partner may even be someone who's also on a weight loss journey.

6. Personal Trainer
A professional, accredited trainer to help you regularly exercise, burn fat, tone up and possibly advise you on food choices. Remember, muscle is heavier than fat, so it's important to get your measurements taken at the start of your exercise plan and regularly each month thereafter.

7. Nutritionist

A qualified specialist in nutrition and the nutritive value of various foods, who can advise you on food and nutrition to support your health, foods you should avoid, combinations of foods that can be useful and those which aren't. A nutritionist can also recommend varieties of foods you hadn't even thought of.

8. Weight Loss Coach

A professionally qualified person like myself who has years of successfully guiding and coaching clients to meet their weight loss goals.

Important note about Accountability Coaches – when it comes to any sort of Accountability Coach, it's VITAL that you're clear on your own personal goals of:
A. what you want them to help you achieve
B. how you would need them to support you

Do some research into who you think might be able to support you, have your questions ready and have a chat with them before committing to anything.

The relationship between an accountability coach and the client must be one of trust, dependability, understanding, and compassion.

You also want to have a sense that your partner is going to be able to support you because they have the knowledge, expertise, experience, and healthy robustness to challenge you when you think you can't do something. You would want them to be able to help you see things from a different perspective which will support you in creating significant positive shifts in your progress.

Sometimes, they may say the things you don't want to hear! What I mean is you might be feeling like giving up or that you're not able to lift a certain weight, for example, and they're confident enough and experienced enough to be able to safely tell you, "Yes, you can!"

So before you commit, ask a lot of questions and check out the reviews from other clients.

It's imperative that you feel that you're investing in a tried and tested, safe pair of hands and someone who's confident enough to appropriately challenge you if necessary!

SELF INVESTMENT STEPS

Go to your Journal and write down how you're going to stay accountable.
What are you going to do?
How are you going to go about doing it?
When are you going to do it?
Commit to it.
And take the action steps to follow up on that!

CHAPTER 22

WILLPOWER

You might think that you're a master at willpower – until you're truly tested. And suddenly, all that will and all that power goes flying out the window. Only to be replaced by a more primitive form of desire, which seems impossible to control.

On the other end of the scale, you might think you've no willpower at all. So you make excuses and slide into bad habits all too easily because you think you can't help it.

Either way, relying on willpower alone is a dangerous approach. Simply using willpower means that no matter how badly you desire something, you're determined to ensure you don't give in. It can feel like you're white-knuckling it, though. The experience is far from enjoyable, and you'll probably cave at some point.

So what is the alternative? How can you lose weight without willpower?

It's very much about recognising the prison your mind has been keeping you in. When someone's in prison, they're locked in and follow daily routines. Many of us are locked into a self-prescribed, repetitive way of thinking that's keeping us stuck in a prison of our own thoughts. With self-awareness and the appropriate helpful mindtools, you have the keys to get out of your prison forever – and this isn't just about your weight loss mindset – these are tools you can use in every aspect of your life.

I've drawn together Mindset Techniques to override the need for willpower. I've included a couple of them in previous chapters, and I'm also including them here. They're so powerful, and as I mentioned in the introduction, you don't have to follow this course sequentially.

You may find that you want to apply all ten steps to your life, or some might appeal to you more than others. However, know this – whatever you plant in your mind and nourish with repetition will become your reality!

SELF INVESTMENT STEPS

1. MINDSET and MAKING MAGICAL MIND LEAPS . As soon as I open my eyes in the morning, I remember to be grateful for all the blessings in my life, and I then set my mind on how I intend to feel today – and I don't leave it to chance: I've already decided what things I want to have in my life and I have an A4 chart stuck up next to my bed on which I've drawn pictures of everything I'm intent on manifesting. (Important point to note here: When I originally drew the chart, I asked the Universe to provide these things to me or something better and gave thanks that it would be so. This is a very vital step to initiate this process.)

So I look at each of the pictures individually in turn, and I imagine that they've already occurred in my life, and I'm gratefully celebrating the result. I experience joy, delight and celebration in my mind! It's important to note here that I'm not asking the Universe to provide it – I think I've already received it. That's the mindset you want for the rest of the day. It doesn't matter that you're not yet your ideal weight and shape. What matters is that you *feel* as if you already are! That's the magical Mind Leap! I've referred to this type of visualisation in previous chapters, and I'm alluding to it again because it's reinforcing a powerful tool you have in your mental toolbox that you've likely not been using in this way. You've probably been unconsciously using this powerful tool negatively – regularly thinking negatively about your body, weight, and shape and then wondering why you're stuck in a loop! Changing that mindset may seem alien at first, but the more you do it, the more it becomes your habit and default state.

I've also stuck little stars around my home and office. They're quite subtle and discreet, but every time I see them, it reminds me to check in with myself and ensure I'm still experiencing that same state of joy and positivity, and if I'm not, then I make the mental adjustments to return me to that state. This might sound a bit mad, but your subconscious will support you in this and give you the appropriate thoughts, choices and actions to create whatever your intention is.

Now, the next thing I'm going to say is REALLY IMPORTANT to know:

When you start to practise this technique, you may find that when you check in with yourself, your mindset is far off from the happy state of mind that you were promising yourself – you may find that you've slipped into an old, familiar negative thought routine. When you realise this, it throws light on why your previous weight loss outcomes have not been successful! You have been unconsciously creating failure by having that negative attitude as your default state. At the very moment you become aware of this, you start the process of creating your new reality! The only difference between an aware and unaware person is that the aware person creates their reality consciously, and the unaware person creates their reality unconsciously. Which are you?

2. TIME. With the Mind Leap technique, you're consistently programming your mind, so over time, the happy and healthy thoughts about yourself become your emotional blueprint and your natural default state. The sense of self-belief and self-empowerment it gives you makes it so much easier to choose healthier habits. And it's self-perpetuating – the better you feel, the healthier choices you make, the healthier the choices you make, the better you feel, and so on ... Using willpower for weight loss becomes a thing of the past.

3. DAYDREAMING. Stop Doing and become just Being. What I mean by this is - enjoy using your imagination to picture yourself

100

as your ideal weight and shape. Let your mind wander – see yourself in various situations BEING your ideal self - what are you doing, what are you wearing, how are you moving, etc. Become aware of the associated happy thoughts and feelings....

As I mentioned in the Visualisations Chapter 4, everything we create happens twice – first in our imagination and then in our actual lives. So, if you can allow yourself to exist as your ideal weight and shape in your mind, then it's going to be much easier for that person to exist in your reality. Make this a daily practice – I often do it once I've turned the lights out at night – it helps me slide into sleep in a very happy state and also programmes my subconscious mind in a very positive and potent way.

4. You can support yourself further by regularly listening to my Meditation Visualisation.

5 (a)   Remind yourself daily of your WHYs. What are the reasons you decided to buy this book? What was it about your life that just had to change?
See your notes on Chapter 1 for a reminder. As you go through this book, you'll likely find that you want to amend or add to your Whys. Originally, your Whys may have been very practical, but with the insights and self-awareness that you're hopefully experiencing on this journey, you may now be finding that the sense of personal development, self-empowerment and peace is something you want to learn more of and develop.

5 (b)   I'd like to think that you're becoming aware of experiencing a broader and more philosophical view of your life – less caught up in sweating the small stuff and more able to question and challenge things that may have upset or triggered you in the past. For example:

You find that you've eaten something you wish you hadn't. Previously, you'd have viewed this as an act of sabotage; it would have made you feel rubbish, and you'd likely give up (again)! However, now you have tools to be able to see it in context – the self-awareness, self-care and self-compassion to make you pause and wonder WHY you ate it (think of the language point 'should/could' that I refer to in Chapter 6) - were you too hungry, did someone offer you something and it would have been rude to refuse, was there absolutely no other choice, or is there some other reason? What's key here is that you get the WHY - the reason for the action, rather than see it as an act of failure, so you can re-assess the situation and apply any mental and emotional adjustments and/or strategies that you may need to support yourself and body-swerve it in the future!

6. The "I'm a failure" language.

We can all have slip-ups, but in previous moments when you've succumbed to temptation, your self-talk might have been, "Oh, I've failed. I'm a failure. I can't stick to a diet. I can't do this". But are you really a failure? That's a very broad-brush statement. You might have had a lapse, but does that brand you a failure? Are you a failure in life? Are you a failure as a friend? Are you a failure as a family member? Are you a failure at work? Are you a failure at keeping a roof over your head? The answer to all or many of these questions is likely to be no. You're actually a success.

Seeing your life in terms of your successes puts your lapse into a different perspective, and you can start to view it from a power-based point-of-view that diminishes its negative charge. You achieved your successes in life because you're strong and resilient – it wasn't all plain sailing, and where you met with failure, you didn't give up. Applying this perception can expand your mind dynamically to support you with newfound resolve in turning things around in your weight loss world.

As I stated in the Affirmations chapter, over the years, you've spent a great deal of time, thought, and energy thinking negative thoughts about your weight and weight loss endeavours. Look where it's got you.

Now it's time to shake off that thinking, wake up to your power and start singing your praises and blowing your trumpet. From that point of view, you can acknowledge that you had a slip-up, but it's no longer a failure.

7. Re-charging Your Mindset – Your Personal Elevator Pitch!

In your secret inner world – that place where your secret self-talk can be harsh and unforgiving, start re-writing the script:

Consider - What are your wins in life? What are you proud of? What have you done that's remarkable? What are you uniquely good at? What projects have you successfully accomplished?

Take the time, dig deep and start putting together your very own personal 'Elevator Pitch':

Organise your mind around how you're going to do this – you can start by making categories – for example, career, business, relationships, friendships, family, parenthood, sporting, home, critical thinking, your personality …

Get it out of your head by writing it down, then edit it down to 30-60 seconds and practise it out loud - like it's a pitch. Regularly speak it out loud to yourself in the mirror – you're selling yourself to yourself. Your positive qualities, your unique qualities. I say mine at the bus stop, in the car, when I'm out and about – especially when I feel challenged. And, of course, you don't always have to say it out loud. You can just think about it.

Here's mine, "I'm Gillian – life hasn't been easy – I've faced heartbreak, loss, hardship, homelessness and substance abuse. However, I've come through all of that and found happiness because I'm smart, strong, patient, persistent, adaptable, able, worthy, loving and lovable. And I've learnt self-compassion."

So what's yours?

103

8. Finding your Super-Power Quality

What's your superpower? What's the quality that has got you through your life through thick and thin, ups and downs, happy and sad? Mine's adaptability. Today, I had a client and hers was Accomplishment. Another client had Perseverance. Think about your life - what's the thread in your personality that keeps recurring to keep you going forward in your life? Once you identify it - and it can take some time and deep thought - you now have an active life tool that you can apply to every situation.

For example, if I'm met with a challenge in my life, I bring out the 'adaptability tool' and ask myself - "How would adaptability handle this challenge or situation?". It instantly starts to expand my thinking, refers me back to how I've managed before and calms me down - because I remember how well being adaptable has helped me manage in the past. This gives me the confidence, belief and mindset I need to advance. So, what's your super-power quality? And how can you apply that tool to your weight loss journey?

You may find it helpful to chat this with someone close, someone you've known for a long time, to get their opinion on the main aspect of your personality that's got you through the highs and lows of your life.

9. Super Booster (1)

Here's an incredibly powerful tool to turbo-boost your sense of your fabulousness!!! Ask your friends and loved ones to use three words to describe different positive aspects of your personality – likely, you're going to hear some very kind and flattering words. Words that you never even considered people had thought about you! Make a list of them and stick them somewhere you'll see them often. I have mine stuck next to my computer so I regularly see them. They reinforce my positive sense of myself – especially in those moments when I need a boost, my eyes are drawn to the wonderful words.

10. Super Booster (2)

Make a list of 31 positive adjectives about yourself – think hard – there'll be plenty, but as I've mentioned before, we're generally not drawn to describing ourselves positively or singing our praises. So here are some examples: caring, loving, genuine, generous, charismatic, daring, clever, intelligent, helpful, honest, strong, reliable, faithful, peaceful, and there'll be many more. Once you have 31, write each one on a separate piece of paper, fold them and put them in a bowl. Each day thereafter, choose one of the pieces of paper at random and read the word it contains. That word is your personal Mantra for that day. Own it, think about it, repeat it often. Consciously percolate your whole day with the beautiful essence of this word. The word represents an aspect of your lovely authentic self, and this is a way of building and strengthening that connection.

To conclude this Chapter, let me give you a life lesson:

It's impossible to be in prison unless we put ourselves in there. This book has provided you with the keys to set yourself free.

CHAPTER 23

MISCELLANEOUS TIPS

Six mind hacks to trick your thinking.

1. How colour can affect your appetite.

Certain colours can stimulate appetite. Fast food chains know all about this and often use red and yellow in their branding and packaging. Bright red excites and stimulates the appetite and encourages people to be impulsive and eat more. Yellow elicits a feeling of comfort.

The colours green and blue are less likely to stimulate appetite. Blue is actually known to suppress appetite and reduce hunger. Simply put, it's the most unappetising colour. Green imparts a feeling of cheerfulness and a relaxing atmosphere. It's also associated with nature and inspires diners to eat healthily,

2. Create an optical illusion.

Using a smaller plate tricks your mind into thinking that you are eating more than you actually are.

3. Use Mindfulness to slow down your eating.

Eating mindfully means that you are fully engaged in the process of eating. It's not incidental to watching TV, scrolling the net or reading. Eating mindfully slows down the eating process and means that you tend to eat more slowly, giving your mind and body, brain and belly, conscious and subconscious mind a chance to simultaneously indicate to you when you are comfortably full and can just stop eating.

4. Know that diet sodas are fooling your mind and body and lead you into wanting more sweet things like sugary snacks.

5. Changing your Cravings.

Yale University School of Medicine recently ran a study in which people were trained to think about the positive attributes of healthy foods. The researchers told them, for instance, to repeatedly tell themselves that broccoli was crunchy and delicious and that if they ate it, they'd feel good about themselves. The results were striking: They found that they could actually get people to increase their cravings for healthy foods!

In a second study, the team trained people to engage in that same type of repeated positive thinking. They discovered that if people practised looking at healthy foods and considering their wonderful qualities, it helped them to make better dietary choices and eat fewer calories per day.

It works the other way too. The studies showed that people can substantially reduce cravings for, say, cakes by thinking of all the negatives connected to eating them – like how they'll fill their blood vessels with fats and diminish their energy, weight gain, blood sugar problems and an increased risk of heart disease, etc. The researchers found that the participants were less inclined to want to eat unhealthy foods and had reduced activity in the part of the brain that's active during cravings.

6. Using psychology in your kitchen

Clear or re-organise your kitchen cabinets and fridge. The magic of getting rid of foods that don't serve you cannot be underestimated. At the minimum, you won't have to deal with temptation in your home! If there are items you cannot throw out because other people who share your space use them, then place them on a shelf in your fridge or cupboards out of your direct line of vision or places/cupboards/drawers you don't normally use.

Supermarkets are well aware of the psychology of product placement – they'll place items they want you to buy at eye level and items they're not so interested in selling on lower or higher shelves! Product placement is effective because it taps into the viewer's emotions and subconscious. So get wise to it and use product placement in your own home! Out of sight, out of mind!

SELF INVESTMENT STEPS

1. Consider investing in blue or green plates and bowls and/or adding napkins in blue or green colours. Also, when choosing kitchen or dining area décor.

2. Invest in smaller dinner plates.

3. Become aware of eating mindfully.

So what is Mindful Eating -

It's about consciously slowing down your eating – so that you can savour your food and take time over it! Taking the time to become consciously more aware of the food on the plate, the textures, the colours, the aromas, and the temperature.

If it's finger food, such as a sandwich, how does it feel between your fingers?

If you're using cutlery, become aware of the coolness and smoothness of the utensils. When you add food to the end of the fork or spoon, become aware of the slight increase in weight.

When you bring the food up to your mouth, become aware of the opening of your lips, closing your lips and then the aroma, taste, texture, temperature and flavours of the food as you chew.

Become aware of the goodness in the food – the vitamins, minerals, nutrients, proteins, etc.

Enjoy each mouthful.
Savour each mouthful.

You will more consciously and easily hear the messages that tell you when you're satisfied, comfortably full, replete, and even if there's still food on the plate, you'll be able to leave it – bin it or make it leftovers for another meal.

4. Consider drinking naturally flavoured fizzy water. Or flavour it yourself with things like lemon, mint, cucumber …

5. Have pictures of healthy foods around you – on your fridge, around your workspace, your bathroom mirror, etc and every time you see them, give yourself a good feeling and a positive thought. Thumbs up to that healthy food! In this way, you're programming your subconscious mind and also your brain!

6. Always keep your healthy snacks in a particular place – that becomes your 'Go To' place in your mind when you want to have something.

WRAPPING IT ALL UP!

So, dear one, you've reached the end of this learning experience and self-awakening journey. I trust that you've found many 'golden nuggets' on the way to assist you in the cognitive process of positively and powerfully programming your subconscious mind and having self-mastery over the outcomes you intend to have in your life. It's been a total joy and delight to have been able to share my insights, wisdom and life tools with you.

As I mentioned previously, you can find me on my private Facebook group, 'Weight Loss Without Willpower' – I do weekly 'Lives', and I'm on there most days, so if you post any questions, you can expect a response from me very rapidly.

There's also an online course of the whole book, which you can find on my website www.changewithgillian.com

You may wish to customise your journey of the Weight Loss Without Willpower programme and work with me 121: I offer exclusive coaching - in-person or online – you can experience first hand guidance from me as I navigate you through the modules giving you exclusive insights, tools and heightened awareness to empower your intentions. You will receive my personal guidance as I combine individualised attention to support your personal needs with my unique methods of hypno-healing – a bespoke holistic mind/body technique using hypnotherapy and my intuitive insights to overcome the negative patterns that have been preventing you from reaching your full potentials.

As I said in the introduction, I'm a Clinical Hypnotherapist and Intuitive Life Coach. Weight management is one of my areas of expertise; however, I also offer help and assistance with anxiety, confidence, and much else. My website has plenty of information if you'd like to know more. I offer a free, confidential initial telephone consultation, so get in touch if you'd like to chat. I'm based in Edinburgh, Scotland, and I work globally online.

I also write a regular Blog covering different aspects of building Emotional Resilience, and you'll see my testimonials and 100+ 5-star Google Reviews that I've received.

**Please remember to be kind to yourself –
your inner world creates your outer world.**

May I wish you success, health, love and blessings!

Printed in Great Britain
by Amazon